THE EIGHTEENT[H]
BRUMAIRE

OF

LOUIS BONAPARTE

BY
KARL MARX

———

TRANSLATED BY
DANIEL DE LEON
THIRD EDITION

———

CHICAGO
CHARLES H. KERR & COMPANY
1913

PUBLISHER'S NOTE TO THIRD EDITION

The first edition of this translation was published in New York in 1897. Ten years later we purchased the plates and copyright and brought out an edition in paper covers. The type was small and the printing unattractive, but the demand for the book continues, and we now offer a new edition from new plates. The translation is unchanged except for a few slight verbal corrections, and we are reprinting the introduction by the translator just as originally written. The events of sixteen years have in many ways confirmed his forecast, and the spectacular figure of Theodore Roosevelt now offers a striking parallel to that of Napoleon the Little.

C. H. K.

March, 1913.

TRANSLATOR'S PREFACE

"The Eighteenth Brumaire of Louis Bonaparte" is one of Karl Marx' most profound and most brilliant monographs. It may be considered the best work extant on the philosophy of history, with an eye especially upon the history of the Movement of the Proletariat, together with the bourgeois and other manifestations that accompany the same, and the tactics that such conditions dictate.

The recent populist uprising; the more recent "Debs Movement"; the thousand and one utopian and chimerical notions that are flaring up; the capitalist manœuvres; the hopeless, helpless grasping after straws, that characterize the conduct of the bulk of the working class; all of these, together with the empty-headed, ominous figures that are springing into notoriety for a time and have their day, mark the present period of the Labor Movement in the nation a critical one. The best information acquirable, the best mental training obtainable are requisite to steer through the existing chaos that the death-tainted social system of today creates all around us. To aid in this needed information and mental training, this instructive work is now made accessible to English readers, and is commended to the serious study of the serious.

The teachings contained in this work are hung on an episode in recent French history. With some this fact may detract of its value. A pedantic, supercilious notion is extensively abroad among us that we are an "Anglo-Saxon" nation; and an equally pedantic, supercilious habit causes many to look to England for inspiration, as from a racial birthplace. Nevertheless, for weal or for woe, there is no such thing extant as "Anglo-Saxon"—of all nations, said to be "Anglo-Saxon," in the United States least. What we still have from England, much as appearances may seem to point the other way, is not of our bone-and-marrow, so to speak, but rather partakes of the nature of "importations." We are no more English on account of them than we are Chinese because we all drink tea.

Of all European nations, France is the one to which we come nearest. Besides its republican form of government—the directness of its history, the unity of its actions, the sharpness that marks its internal development, are all characteristics that find their parallel here best, and vice versa. In all essentials the study of modern French history, particularly when sketched by such a master hand as Marx', is the most valuable one for the acquisition of that historic, social and biologic insight that our country stands particularly in need of, and that will be inestimable during the approaching critical days.

For the assistance of those who, unfamiliar with the history of France, may be confused by some of the terms used by Marx, the following explanations may prove aidful:

On the 18th Brumaire (Nov. 9th), the post-revolutionary development of affairs in France enabled the first Napoleon to take a step that led with inevitable certainty to the imperial throne. The circumstance that fifty and odd years later similar events aided his nephew, Louis Bonaparte, to take a similar step with a similar result, gives the name to this work—"The Eighteenth Brumaire of Louis Bonaparte."

As to the other terms and allusions that occur, the following sketch will suffice:

Upon the overthrow of the first Napoleon came the restoration of the Bourbon throne (Louis XVIII, succeeded by Charles X). In July, 1830, an uprising of the upper tier of the bourgeoisie, or capitalist class—the aristocracy of finance—, overthrew the Bourbon throne, or landed aristocracy, and set up the throne of Orleans, a younger branch of the house of Bourbon, with Louis Philippe as king. From the month in which this revolution occurred, Louis Philippe's monarchy is called the "July Monarchy." In February, 1848, a revolt of a lower tier of the capitalist class—the industrial bourgeoisie—, against the aristocracy of finance, in turn dethroned Louis Philippe. This affair, also named from the month in which it took place, is the "February Revolution." The "Eighteenth Brumaire" starts with that event.

Despite the inapplicableness to our own affairs of the political names and political leadership herein described, both these names and leaderships are to such an extent the products of an economic-social development that has here too taken place with even greater sharpness, and they have their present or threatened counterparts here so completely, that, by the light of this work of Marx', we are best enabled to understand our own history, to know whence we come, whither we are going and how to conduct ourselves.

D. D. L.

New York, Sept. 12, 1897.

THE EIGHTEENTH BRUMAIRE
OF
LOUIS BONAPARTE

I.

Hegel says somewhere that all great historic facts and personages recur twice. He forgot to add: "Once as tragedy, and again as farce." Caussidiere for Danton, Louis Blanc for Robespierre, the "Mountain" of 1848-51 for the "Mountain" of 1793-05, the Nephew for the Uncle. The identical caricature marks also the conditions under which the second edition of the eighteenth Brumaire is issued.

Man makes his own history, but he does not make it out of the whole cloth; he does not make it out of conditions chosen by himself, but out of such as he finds close at hand. The tradition of all past generations weighs like an alp upon the brain of the living. At the very time when men appear engaged in revolutionizing things and themselves, in bringing about what never was before, at such very epochs of revolutionary crisis do they anxiously conjure up into their service the spirits of the past, assume their names, their battle cries, their costumes to enact a new historic scene in such time-honored disguise and with such borrowed language. Thus did Luther masquerade as the Apostle Paul; thus did the revolution of 1789-1814 drape itself, alternately as Roman Republic and as Roman Empire; nor did the revolution of 1848 know what better to do than to parody at one time the year 1789, at another the revolutionary traditions of 1793-95. Thus does the beginner, who has acquired a new language, keep on translating it back into his own mother tongue; only then has he grasped the spirit of the new language and is able freely to express himself therewith when he moves in it without recollections of the old, and has forgotten in its use his own hereditary tongue.

When these historic conjurations of the dead past are closely observed a striking difference is forthwith noticeable. Camille Desmoulins, Danton, Robespierre, St. Juste, Napoleon, the heroes as well as the parties and the masses of the old French revolution, achieved in Roman costumes and with Roman phrases the task of their time: the emancipation and the establishment of modern bourgeois society. One set knocked to pieces the old feudal groundwork and mowed down the feudal heads that had grown upon it; Napoleon brought about, within France, the conditions under which alone free competition could develop, the partitioned lands be exploited, the nation's unshackled powers of industrial production be utilized; while, beyond the French frontier, he swept away everywhere the establishments of feudality, so far as requisite, to furnish the bourgeois social system of France with fit surroundings of the European continent, and such as were in keeping with the times. Once the new social establishment was set on foot, the antediluvian giants vanished, and, along with them, the resuscitated Roman world — the Brutuses, Gracchi, Publicolas, the Tribunes, the Senators, and Cæsar himself. In its sober reality, bourgeois society had produced its own true interpreters in the Says, Cousins, Royer-Collards, Benjamin Constants and Guizots; its real generals sat behind the office desks; and the mutton-head of Louis XVIII. was its political head. Wholly absorbed in the production of wealth and in the peaceful fight of competition, this society could no longer understand that the ghosts of the days of Rome had watched over its cradle. And yet, lacking in heroism as bourgeois society is, it nevertheless had stood in need of heroism, of self-sacrifice, of terror, of civil war, and of bloody battle fields to bring it into the world. Its gladiators found in the stern classic traditions of the Roman republic the ideals and the form, the self-deceptions, that they needed in order to conceal from themselves the narrow bourgeois substance of their own struggles, and to keep their passion up to the height of a great historic tragedy. Thus, at another stage of development, a century before, did Cromwell and the English people draw from the Old Testament the language, passions and illusions for their own bourgeois revolution. When the real goal was reached, when the remodeling of English society was accomplished, Locke supplanted Habakuk.

Accordingly, the reviving of the dead in those revolutions served the purpose of glorifying the new struggles, not of parodying the old; it served the purpose of exaggerating to the imagination the given task, not to recoil before its practical solution; it served the purpose of rekindling the revolutionary spirit, not to trot out its ghost.

In 1848-51 only the ghost of the old revolution wandered about, from Marrast the *"Républicain en gaunts jaunes,"*[1] who disguised himself in old Bailly, down to the adventurer, who hid his repulsively trivial features under the iron death mask of Napoleon. A whole people, that imagines it has imparted to itself accelerated powers of motion through a revolution, suddenly finds itself transferred back to a dead epoch, and, lest there be any mistake possible on this head, the old dates turn up again; the old calendars; the old names; the old edicts, which long since had sunk to the level of the antiquarian's learning; even the old bailiffs, who had long seemed mouldering with decay. The nation takes on the appearance of that crazy Englishman in Bedlam, who imagines he is living in the days of the Pharaohs, and daily laments the hard work that he must do in the Ethiopian mines as gold digger, immured in a subterranean prison, with a dim lamp fastened on his head, behind him the slave overseer with a long whip, and, at the mouths of the mine a mob of barbarous camp servants who understand neither the convicts in the mines nor one another, because they do not speak a common language. "And all this," cries the crazy Englishman, "is demanded of me, the free-born Englishman, in order to make gold for old Pharaoh." "In order to pay off the debts of the Bonaparte family"—sobs the French nation.

---

[1] Silk-stocking republican.

The Englishman, so long as he was in his senses, could not rid himself of the rooted thought of making gold. The Frenchmen, so long as they were busy with a revolution, could not rid themselves of the Napoleonic memory, as the election of December 10th proved. They longed to escape from the dangers of revolution back to the flesh pots of Egypt; the 2d of December, 1851, was the answer. They have not merely the caricature of the old Napoleon, but the old Napoleon himself—caricatured as he needs must appear in the middle of the nineteenth century.

The social revolution of the nineteenth century can not draw its poetry from the past, it can draw that only from the future. It cannot start upon its work before it has stricken off all superstition concerning the past. Former revolutions required historic reminiscences in order to intoxicate themselves with their own issues. The revolution of the nineteenth century must let the dead bury their dead in order to reach its issue. With the former, the phrase surpasses the substance; with this one, the substance surpasses the phrase.

The February revolution was a surprisal; old society was taken unawares; and the people proclaimed this political stroke a great historic act whereby the new era was opened. On the 2d of December, the February revolution is jockeyed by the trick of a false player, and what is seen to be overthrown is no longer the monarchy, but the liberal concessions which had been wrung from it by centuries of struggles. Instead of society itself having conquered a new point, only the State appears to have returned to its oldest form, to the simply brazen rule of the sword and the club. Thus, upon the "coup de main" of February, 1848, comes the response of the "coup de téte" of December, 1851. So won, so lost. Meanwhile, the interval did not go by unutilized. During the years 1848-1851, French society retrieved in abbreviated, because revolutionary, method the lessons and teachings, which—if it was to be more than a disturbance of the surface—should have preceded the February revolution, had it developed in regular order, by rule, so to say. Now French society seems to have receded behind its point of departure; in fact, however, it was compelled to first produce its own revolutionary point of departure, the situation, circumstances, conditions, under which alone the modern revolution is in earnest.

Bourgeois revolutions, like those of the eighteenth century, rush onward rapidly from success to success, their stage effects outbid one another, men and things seem to be set in flaming brilliants, ecstasy is the prevailing spirit; but they are short-lived, they reach their climax speedily, then society relapses into a long fit of nervous reaction before it learns how to appropriate the fruits of its period of feverish excitement. Proletarian revolutions, on the contrary, such as those of the nineteenth century, criticize themselves constantly; constantly interrupt themselves in their own course; come back to what seems to have been accomplished, in order to start over anew; scorn with cruel thoroughness the half measures, weaknesses and meannesses of their first attempts; seem to throw down their adversary only in order to enable him to draw fresh strength from the earth, and again to rise up against them in more gigantic stature; constantly recoil in fear before the undefined monster magnitude of their own objects—until finally that situation is created which renders all retreat impossible, and the conditions themselves cry out: "Hic Rhodus, hic salta!"[2]

Every observer of average intelligence, even if he failed to follow step by step the course of French development, must have anticipated that an unheard of fiasco was in store for the revolution. It was enough to hear the self-satisfied yelpings of victory wherewith the Messieurs Democrats mutually congratulated one another upon the pardons of May 2d, 1852. Indeed, May 2d had become a fixed idea in their heads: it had become a dogma with them—something like the day on which Christ was to reappear and the Millennium to begin had formed in the heads of the Chiliasts. Weakness had, as it ever does, taken refuge in the wonderful; it believed the enemy was overcome if, in its imagination, it hocus-pocused him away; and it lost all sense of the present in the imaginary apotheosis of the future, that was at hand, and of the deeds, that it had "in petto," but which it did not yet want to bring to the scratch. The heroes, who ever seek to refute their established incompetence by mutually bestowing their sympathy upon one another and by pulling together, had packed their satchels, taken their laurels in advance payments and were just engaged in the work of getting discounted "in partibus," on the stock exchange, the republics for which, in the silence of their unassuming dispositions, they had carefully organ-

---

2 Here is Rhodes, leap here! An allusion to Æsop's Fables.

ized the government personel. The 2d of December struck them like a bolt from a clear sky; and the peoples, who, in periods of timid despondency, gladly allow their hidden fears to be drowned by the loudest screamers, will perhaps have become convinced that the days are gone by when the cackling of geese could save the Capitol.

The constitution, the national assembly, the dynastic parties, the blue and the red republicans, the heroes from Africa, the thunder from the tribune, the flash-lightnings from the daily press, the whole literature, the political names and the intellectual celebrities, the civil and the criminal law, the "liberté, egalité, fraternité," together with the 2d of May, 1852,—all vanished like a phantasmagoria before the ban of one man, whom his enemies themselves do not pronounce an adept at witchcraft. Universal suffrage seems to have survived only for a moment, to the end that, before the eyes of the whole world, it should make its own testament with its own hands, and, in the name of the people, declare: "All that exists deserves to perish."

It is not enough to say, as the Frenchmen do, that their nation was taken by surprise. A nation, no more than a woman, is excused for the unguarded hour when the first adventurer who comes along can do violence to her. The riddle is not solved by such shifts, it is only formulated in other words. There remains to be explained how a nation of thirty-six millions can be surprised by three swindlers, and taken to prison without resistance.

Let us recapitulate in general outlines the

phases which the French revolution of February 24th, 1848, to December, 1851, ran through.

Three main periods are unmistakable:

First—The February period;

Second—The period of constituting the republic, or of the constitutive national assembly (May 4, 1848, to May 29th, 1849);

Third—The period of the constitutional republic, or of the legislative national assembly (May 29, 1849, to December 2, 1851).

The first period, from February 24, or the downfall of Louis Philippe, to May 4, 1848, the date of the assembling of the constitutive assembly—the February period proper—may be designated as the prologue of the revolution. It officially expressed its own character in this, that the government which it improvised declared itself "provisional;" and, like the government, everything that was broached, attempted or uttered, pronounced itself provisional. Nobody and nothing dared to assume the right of permanent existence and of an actual fact. All the elements that had prepared or determined the revolution—dynastic opposition, republican bourgeoise, democratic-republican small traders' class, social-democratic labor element—all found "provisionally" their place in the February government.

It could not be otherwise. The February days contemplated originally a reform of the suffrage laws, whereby the area of the politically privileged among the property-holding class was to be extended, while the exclusive rule of the aristocracy of finance was to be overthrown. When, however, it came to a real conflict, when the people

mounted the barricades, when the National Guard
stood passive, when the army offered no serious
resistance, and the kingdom ran away, then the
republic seemed self-understood. Each party in-
terpreted it in its own sense. Won, arms in hand,
by the proletariat, they put upon it the stamp of
their own class, and proclaimed the social republic.
Thus the general purpose of modern revolutions
was indicated, a purpose, however, that stood in
most singular contradiction to every thing that,
with the material at hand, with the stage of en-
lightenment that the masses had reached, and
under existing circumstances and conditions,
could be immediately used. On the other hand,
the claims of all the other elements, that had
co-operated in the revolution of February, were
recognized by the lion's share that they received
in the government. Hence, in no period do we
find a more motley mixture of high-sounding
phrases together with actual doubt and helpless-
ness; of more enthusiastic reform aspirations, together with a more slavish adherence to the old
routine; more seeming harmony permeating the
whole of society together with a deeper alienation
of its several elements. While the Parisian proletariat was still gloating over the sight of the
great perspective that had disclosed itself to their
view, and was indulging in seriously meant dis-
cussions over the social problems, the old powers
of society had groomed themselves, had gathered
together, had deliberated and found an unexpected support in the mass of the nation—the peasants
and small traders—all of whom threw themselves
on a sudden upon the political stage, after the
barriers of the July monarchy had fallen down.

The second period, from May 4, 1848, to the
end of May, 1849, is the period of the constitution, of the founding of the bourgeois republic.
Immediately after the February days, not only
was the dynastic opposition surprised by the republicans, and the republicans by the Socialists,
but all France was surprised by Paris. The
national assembly, that met on May 4, 1848, to
frame a constitution, was the outcome of the national elections; it represented the nation. It
was a living protest against the assumption of the
February days, and it was intended to bring the
results of the revolution back to the bourgeois
measure. In vain did the proletariat of Paris,
which forthwith understood the character of this
national assembly, endeavor, a few days after its
meeting, on May 15, to deny its existence by
force, to dissolve it, to disperse the organic ap-
parition, in which the reacting spirit of the nation was threatening them, and thus reduce it
back to its separate component parts. As is
known, the 15th of May had no other result than
that of removing Blanqui and his associates, i. e.,
the real leaders of the proletarian party, from
the public scene for the whole period of the cycle
which we are here considering.

Upon the bourgeois monarchy of Louis
Philippe, only the bourgeois republic could follow; that is to say, a limited portion of the bourgeoisie having ruled under the name of the king,
now the whole bourgeoisie was to rule under the
name of the people. The demands of the Parisian
proletariat are utopian tom-fooleries that have to
be done away with. To this declaration of the
constitutional national assembly, the Paris pro-

letariat answers with the June insurrection, the most colossal event in the history of European civil wars. The bourgeois republic won. On its side stood the aristocracy of finance, the industrial bourgeoisie; the middle class; the small traders' class; the army; the slums, organized as Guarde Mobile; the intellectual celebrities, the parsons' class, and the rural population. On the side of the Parisian proletariat stood none but itself. Over 3,000 insurgents were massacred, after the victory 15,000 were transported without trial. With this defeat, the proletariat steps to the background on the revolutionary stage. It always seeks to crowd forward, so soon as the movement seems to acquire new impetus, but with ever weaker effort and ever smaller results. So soon as any of the above lying layers of society gets into revolutionary fermentation, it enters into alliance therewith and thus shares all the defeats which the several parties successively suffer. But these succeeding blows become ever weaker the more generally they are distributed over the whole surface of society. The more important leaders of the Proletariat, in its councils, and the press, fall one after another victims of the courts, and ever more questionable figures step to the front. *It partly throws itself upon doctrinaire experiments, "co-operative banking" and "labor exchange" schemes: in other words, it goes into movements, in which it gives up the task of revolutionizing the old world with its own large collective weapons and on the contrary, seeks to bring about its emancipation, behind the back of society, in private ways, within the narrow bounds of its own class conditions, and, con-*

sequently, inevitably fails. The proletariat seems
to be able neither to find again the revolutionary
magnitude within itself nor to draw new energy
from the newly formed alliances until *all the
classes,* with whom it contended in June, shall
lie prostrate along with itself. But in all these
defeats, the proletariat succumbs at least with the
honor that attaches to great historic struggles;
not France alone, all Europe trembles before the
June earthquake, while the successive defeats in-
flicted upon the the higher classes are bought so
easily that they need the brazen exaggeration of
the victorious party itself to be at all able to
pass muster as an event; and these defeats become more disgraceful the further removed the
defeated party stands from the proletariat.

True enough, the defeat of the June insurgents
prepared, leveled the ground, upon which the
bourgeois republic could be founded and erected;
but it, at the same time, showed that there are
in Europe other issues besides that of "Republic
or Monarchy." It revealed the fact that here
the Bourgeois Republic meant the unbridled despotism of one class over another. It proved that,
with nations enjoying an older civilization, having developed class distinctions, modern conditions of production, an intellectual consciousness,
wherein all traditions of old have been dissolved
through the work of centuries, that with such
countries the republic means only the *political
revolutionary form of bourgeois society,* not its
conservative form of existence, as is the case in
the United States of America, where, true
enough, the classes already exist, but have not
yet acquired permanent character, are in constant

flux and reflux, constantly changing their elements and yielding them up to one another; where the modern means of production, instead of coinciding with a stagnant population, rather compensate for the relative scarcity of heads and hands; and, finally, where the feverishly youthful life of material production, which has to appropriate a new world to itself, has so far left neither time nor opportunity to abolish the illusions of old. [3]

All classes and parties joined hands in the June days in a "Party of Order" against the class of the proletariat, which was designated as the "Party of Anarchy," of Socialism, of Communism. They claimed to have "saved" society against the "enemies of society." They gave out the slogans of the old social order—"Property, Family, Religion, Order"—as the pass-words for their army, and cried out to the counter-revolutionary crusaders: "In this sign thou wilt conquer!" From that moment on, so soon as any of the numerous parties, which had marshalled themselves under this sign against the June insurgents, tries, in turn, to take the revolutionary field in the interest of its own class, it goes down in its turn before the cry: "Property, Family, Religion, Order." Thus it happens that "society is saved" as often as the circle of its ruling class is narrowed, as often as a more exclusive interest asserts itself over the general. Every demand for the most simple bourgeois financial reform, for the most ordinary liberalism, for the most commonplace republicanism, for the flattest democracy, is forthwith punished as

---

[3] This was written at the beginning of 1852.

an "assault upon society," and is branded as
"Socialism." Finally the High Priests of "Religion and Order" themselves are kicked off their
tripods; are fetched out of their beds in the dark,
hurried into patrol wagons, thrust into jail or
sent into exile; their temple is razed to the
ground, their mouths are sealed, their pen is
broken, their law torn to pieces in the name of
Religion, of Family, of Property, and of Order.
Bourgeois, fanatic on the point of "Order," are
shot down on their own balconies by drunken
soldiers, forfeit their family property, and their
houses are bombarded for pastime—all in the
name of Property, of Family, of Religion, and
of Order. Finally, the refuse of bourgeois society
constitutes the "holy phalanx of Order," and the
hero Crapulinsky makes his entry into the Tuileries as the "Savior of Society."

II.

Let us resume the thread of events.

The history of the Constitutional National
Assembly from the June days on, is the history
of the supremacy and dissolution of the republican bourgeois party, the party which is known
under the several names of "Tricolor Republican," "True Republican," "Political Republican,"
"Formal Republican," etc., etc.

Under the bourgeois monarchy of Louis
Philippe, this party had constituted the Official
Republican Opposition, and consequently had
been a recognized element in the then political
world. It had its representatives in the Cham-

bers, and commanded considerable influence in
the press. Its Parisian organ, the "National,"
passed, in its way, for as respectable a paper as
the "Journal des Debats." This position in the
constitutional monarchy corresponded to its character. The party was not a fraction of the bourgeoisie, held together by great and common interests, and marked by special business requirements. It was a coterie of bourgeois with republican ideas—writers, lawyers, officers and
civil employees, whose influence rested upon the
personal antipathies of the country for Louis
Philippe, upon reminiscences of the old Republic, upon the republican faith of a number of
enthusiasts, and, above all, upon the spirit of
French patriotism, whose hatred of the treaties
of Vienna and of the alliance with England kept
them perpetually on the alert. The "National"
owed a large portion of its following under Louis
Philippe to this covert imperialism, that, later,
under the republic, could stand up against it as a
deadly competitor in the person of Louis Bonaparte. The paper fought the aristocracy of
finance just the same as did the rest of the bourgeois opposition. The polemic against the budget,
which, in France, was closely connected with the
opposition to the aristocracy of finance, furnished
too cheap a popularity and too rich a material
for Puritanical leading articles, not to be exploited. The industrial bourgeoisie was thankful
to it for its servile defence of the French tariff
system, which, however, the paper had taken up
more out of patriotic than economic reasons; the
whole bourgeois class was thankful to it for its
vicious denunciations of Communism and Social-

ism. For the rest, the party of the "National"
was *purely republican,* i. e., it demanded a republican instead of a monarchic form of bourgeois
government; above all, it demanded for the bourgeoisie the lion's share of the government. As
to how this transformation was to be accomplished, the party was far from being clear. What,
however, was clear as day to it and was openly
declared at the reform banquets during the last
days of Louis Philippe's reign, was its unpopu-
larity with the democratic middle class, especially
with the revolutionary proletariat. These pure
republicans, as pure republicans go, were at first
on the very point of contenting themselves with
the regency of the Duchess of Orleans, when the
February revolution broke out, and when it gave
their best known representatives a place in the
provisional government. Of course, they enjoyed
from the start the confidence of the bourgeoisie
and of the majority of the Constitutional National Assembly. The Socialist elements of the
Provisional Government were promptly excluded
from the Executive Committee which the Assembly had elected upon its convening, and the
party of the "National" subsequently utilized the
outbreak of the June insurrection to dismiss this
Executive Committee also, and thus rid itself
of its nearest rivals—the *small traders' class* or
democratic republicans (Ledru-Rollin, etc.). Cavaignac, the General of the bourgeois republican
party, who commanded at the battle of June,
stepped into the place of the Executive Committee with a sort of dictatorial power. Marrast,
former editor-in-chief of the "National", became
permanent President of the Constitutional Na-

tional Assembly, and the Secretaryship of State, together with all the other important posts, devolved upon the pure republicans.

The republican bourgeois party, which since long had looked upon itself as the legitimate heir of the July monarchy, thus found itself surpassed in its own ideal; but it came into power, not as it had dreamed under Louis Philippe, through a liberal revolt of the bourgeoisie against the throne, but through a grape-shot-and-canistered mutiny of the proletariat against Capital. That which it imagined to be the *most revolutionary,* came about as the *most counter-revolutionary* event. The fruit fell into its lap, but it fell from the Tree of Knowledge, not from the Tree of Life.

The exclusive power of the bourgeois republicans lasted only from June 24 to the 10th of December, 1848. It is summed up in the *framing of a republican constitution* and in *the state of siege of Paris.*

The new Constitution was in substance only a republicanized edition of the constitutional charter of 1830. The limited suffrage of the July monarchy, which excluded even a large portion of the bourgeoisie from political power, was irreconcilable with the existence of the bourgeois republic. The February revolution had forthwith proclaimed direct and universal suffrage in the place of the old law. The bourgeois republicans could not annul this act. They had to content themselves with tacking to it the limitation of a six months' residence. The old organization of the administrative law, of municipal government, of court procedures, of the army, etc., remained untouched, or, where the constitution did change them, the change affected their index, not their subject; their name, not their substance.

The inevitable "General Staff" of the "freedoms" of 1848—personal freedom, freedom of the press, of speech, of association and of assemblage, freedom of instruction, of religion, etc.— received a constitutional uniform that rendered them invulnerable. Each of these freedoms is proclaimed the absolute right of the French citizen, but always with the gloss that it is unlimited in so far only as it be not curtailed by the "equal rights of others," and by the "public safety," or by the "laws," which are intended to effect this harmony. For instance:

"Citizens have the right of association, of peaceful and unarmed assemblage, of petitioning, and of expressing their opinions through the press or otherwise. *The enjoyment of these rights has no limitation other than the equal rights of others and the public safety.*" (Chap. II. of the French Constitution, Section 8.)

"Education is free. The freedom of education shall be *enjoyed* under the conditions provided by law, and under the supervision of the State." (Section 9.)

"The domicile of the citizen is inviolable, except under the forms prescribed by law.'" (Chap. I., Section 3), etc., etc.

The Constitution, it will be noticed, constantly alludes to future organic laws, that are to carry out the glosses, and are intended to regulate the enjoyment of these unabridged freedoms, to the end that they collide neither with one another nor with the public safety. Later on, the organic laws are called into existence by the "Friends of Order," and all the above named freedoms are so regulated that, in their enjoyment, the bourgeoisie encounter no opposition from the like rights of the other classes. Wherever the bourgeoisie wholly interdicted these rights to "others," or allowed them their enjoyment under conditions that were but so many police snares, it was always done only in the interest of the "public safety," i. e., of the bourgeoisie, as required by the Constitution.

Hence it comes that both sides—the "Friends of Order," who abolished all those freedoms, as well as the democrats, who had demanded them all—appeal with full right to the Constitution: Each paragraph of the Constitution contains its own antithesis, its own Upper and Lower House —freedom as a generalization, the abolition of freedom as a specification. Accordingly, so long as the *name* of freedom was respected, and only its real enforcement was prevented—in a legal way, of course—the constitutional existence of freedom remained uninjured, untouched, however completely its *common* existence might be extinguished.

This Constitution, so ingeniously made invulnerable, was, however, like Achilles, vulnerable at one point: not in its heel, but in its head, or rather, in the two heads into which it ran out— the Legislative Assembly, on the one hand, and the President on the other. Run through the Constitution and it will be found that only those paragraphs wherein the relation of the President to the Legislative Assembly is defined, are absolute, positive, uncontradictory, undistortable.

Here the bourgeois republicans were concerned in securing their own position. Articles 45-70 of the Constitution are so framed that the National Assembly can constitutionally remove the President, but the President can set aside the National Assembly only unconstitutionally, he can set it aside only by setting aside the Constitution itself. Accordingly, by these provisions, the National Assembly challenges its own violent destruction. It not only consecrates, like the charter of 1830, the division of powers, but it extends this feature to an unbearably contradictory extreme. The "play of constitutional powers," as Guizot styled the clapper-clawings between the legislative and the executive powers, plays permanent "vabanque" in the Constitution of 1848. On the one side, 750 representatives of the people, elected and qualified for re-election by universal suffrage, who constitute an uncontrolable, indissoluble, indivisible National Assembly, a National Assembly that enjoys legislative omnipotence, that decides in the last instance over war, peace and commercial treaties, that alone has the power to grant amnesties, and that, through its perpetuity, continually maintains the foreground on the stage; on the other, a President, clad with all the attributes of royalty, with the right to appoint and remove his ministers independently from the national assembly, holding in his hands all the means of executive power, the dispenser of all posts, and thereby the arbiter of at least one and a half million existences in France, so many being dependent upon the 500,000 civil employes and upon the officers of all grades. He has the whole armed power behind him. He enjoys the privilege of granting pardons to individual criminals; suspending the National Guards; of removing with the consent of the Council of State the general, cantonal and municipal Councilmen, elected by the citizens themselves. The initiative and direction of all negotiations with foreign countries are reserved to him. While the Assembly itself is constantly acting upon the stage, and is exposed to the critically vulgar light of day, he leads a hidden life in the Elysian fields, only with Article 45 of the Constitution before his eyes and in his heart daily calling out to him, *"Frère, il faut mourir!"*[1] Your power expires on the second Sunday of the beautiful month of May, in the fourth year after your election! The glory is then at an end; the play is not performed twice; and, if you have any debts, see to it betimes that you pay them off with the 600,000 francs that the Constitution has set aside for you, unless, perchance, you should prefer traveling to Clichy[2] on the second Monday of the beautiful month of May."

While the Constitution thus clothes the President with actual power, it seeks to secure the moral power to the National Assembly. Apart from the circumstance that it is impossible to create a moral power through legislative paragraphs, the Constitution again neutralizes itself in that it causes the President to be chosen by all the Frenchmen through direct suffrage. While the votes of France are splintered to pieces upon the 750 members of the National Assembly, they are here, on the contrary, concentrated upon *one*

[1] Brother, you must die!
[2] The debtors' prison.

individual. While each separate Representative
represents only this or that party, this or that city,
this or that dunghill, or possibly only the necessity
of electing some one Seven-hundred-and-fiftieth
or other, with whom neither the issue nor the
man is closely considered, that *one*, the President,
on the contrary, is the elect of the nation, and
the act of his election is the trump card, that
the sovereign people plays out once every four
years. The elected National Assembly stands in
a metaphysical, but the elected President in a
personal, relation to the nation. True enough,
the National Assembly presents in its several
Representatives the various sides of the national
spirit, but, in the President, this spirit is incarnated. As against the National Assembly, the
President possesses a sort of divine right, he is
by the grace of the people.

Thetis, the sea-goddess, had prophesied to
Achilles that he would die in the bloom of youth.
The Constitution, which had its weak spot, like
Achilles, had also, like Achilles, the presentiment
that it would depart by premature death. It was
enough for the pure republicans, engaged at the
work of framing a constitution, to cast a glance
from the misty heights of their ideal republic
down upon the profane world in order to realize
how the arrogance of the royalists, of the Bonapartists, of the democrats, of the Communists,
rose daily, together with their own discredit, and
in the same measure as they approached the com-
pletion of their legislative work of art, without
Thetis having for this purpose to leave the sea
and impart the secret to them. They sought to
outwit fate by means of constitutional artifice,

through Section 111 of the Constitution, according to which every motion to revise the Constitution had to be discussed three successive times, between each of which a full month was to elapse, and required at least a three-fourths majority, with the additional proviso that not less than 500 members of the National Assembly voted. They thereby only made the impotent attempt, still to exercise as a parliamentary minority, to which in their mind's eye they prophetically saw themselves reduced, a power, that, at this very time, when they still disposed over the parliamentary majority and over all the machinery of government, was daily slipping from their weak hands.

Finally, the Constitution entrusts itself for safe keeping, in a melodramatic paragraph, "to the watchfulness and patriotism of the whole French people, and of each individual Frenchman," after having just before, in another paragraph, entrusted the "watchful" and the "patriotic" themselves to the tender, inquisitorial attention of the High Court, instituted by itself.

That was the Constitution of 1848, which, on the 2d of December, 1851, was not overthrown by one head, but tumbled down at the touch of a mere hat; though, true enough, that hat was a three-cornered Napoleon hat.

While the bourgeois republicans were engaged in the Assembly with the work of splicing this Constitution, of discussing and voting, Cavaignac, on the outside, maintained the state of siege of Paris. The state of siege of Paris was the midwife of the constitutional assembly, during its republican pains of travail. When the constitution is later on swept off the earth by the bayonet,

it should not be forgotten that it was by the bayonet, likewise—and the bayonet turned against the
people, at that—that it had to be protected in its
mother's womb, and that by the bayonet it had
to be planted on earth. The ancestors of these
"honest republicans" had caused their symbol,
the tricolor, to make the tour of Europe. These,
in their turn also made a discovery, which all of
itself, found its way over the whole continent,
but, with ever renewed love, came back to France,
until, by this time, it had acquired the right of
citizenship in one-half of her Departments—the
state of siege. A wondrous discovery this was,
periodically applied at each succeeding crisis in
the course of the French revolution. But the
barrack and the bivouac, thus periodically laid
on the head of French society, to compress her
brain and reduce her to quiet; the sabre and the
musket, periodically made to perform the func-
tions of judges and of administrators, of guard-
ians and of censors, of police officers and of
watchmen; the military moustache and the soldier's jacket, periodically heralded as the highest wisdom and guiding stars of society;—were
not all of these, the barrack and the bivouac, the
sabre and the musket, the moustache and the soldier's jacket bound, in the end, to hit upon the
idea that they might as well save society once
for all, by proclaiming their own régime as supreme, and relieve bourgeois society wholly of
the care of ruling itself? The barrack and the
bivouac, the sabre and the musket, the moustache
and the soldier's jacket were all the more bound
to hit upon this idea, seeing that they could then
also expect better cash payment for their in-

creased deserts, while at the merely periodic
states of siege and the transitory savings of
society at the behest of this or that bourgeois
faction, very little solid matter fell to them except some dead and wounded, besides some
friendly bourgeois grimaces. Should not the military, finally, in and for its own interest, play the
game of "state of siege," and simultaneously be-
siege the bourgeois exchanges? Moreover, it
must not be forgotten, and be it observed in passing, that Col. Bernard, the same President of the
Military Committee, who, under Cavaignac,
helped to deport 15,000 insurgents without trial,
moves at this period again at the head of the
Military Committees now active in Paris.

Although the honest, the pure republicans built
with the state of siege the nursery in which the
Praetorian guards of December 2, 1851, were
to be reared, they, on the other hand, deserve
praise in that, instead of exaggerating the feeling of patriotism, as under Louis Philippe, now
they themselves are in command of the national
power, they crawl before foreign powers; instead of making Italy free, they allow her to
be reconquered by Austrians and Neapolitans.
The election of Louis Bonaparte for President
on December 10, 1848, put an end to the dictatorship of Cavaignac and to the constitutional assembly.

In Article 44 of the Constitution it is said:
"The President of the French Republic must
never have lost his quality of French citizen."
The first President of the French Republic, L. N.
Bonaparte, had not only lost his quality of
French citizen, had not only been an English

special constable, but was even a naturalized Swiss citizen.

In the previous chapter I have explained the meaning of the election of December 10. I shall not here return to it. Suffice it here to say that it was a *reaction of the farmers' class,* who had been expected to pay the costs of the February revolution, against the other classes of the nation: it was a *reaction of the country against the city.* It met with great favor among the soldiers, to whom the republicans of the "National" had brought neither fame nor funds; among the great bourgeoisie, who hailed Bonaparte as a bridge to the monarchy; and among the proletarians and small traders, who hailed him as a scourge to Cavaignac. I shall later have occasion to enter closer into the relation of the farmers to the French revolution.

The epoch between December 20, 1848, and the dissolution of the constitutional assembly in May, 1849, embraces the history of the downfall of the bourgeois republicans. After they had founded a republic for the bourgeoisie, had driven the revolutionary proletariat from the field, and had meanwhile silenced the democratic middle class, they are themselves shoved aside by the mass of the bourgeoisie, who justly appropriate this republic as their property. This bourgeois mass was *Royalist,* however. A part thereof, the large landed proprietors, had ruled under the restoration, hence, was *Legitimist:* the other part, the aristocrats of finance and the large industrial capitalists, had ruled under the July monarchy, hence, was *Orleanist.* The high functionaries of the Army, of the University, of the Church, in the civil service, of the Academy and of the press, divided themselves on both sides, although in unequal parts. Here, in the bourgeois republic, that bore neither the name of *Bourbon,* nor of *Orleans,* but the name of *Capital,* they had found the form of government under which they could all rule in common. Already the June insurrection had united them all into a "Party of Order." The next thing to do was to remove the bourgeois republicans who still held the seats in the National Assembly. As brutally as these pure republicans had abused their own physical power against the people, so cowardly, low-spirited, disheartened, broken, powerless did they yield, now when the issue was the maintenance of their own republicanism and their own legislative rights against the Executive power and the royalists. I need not here narrate the shameful history of their dissolution. It was not a downfall, it was extinction. Their history is at an end for all time. In the period that follows, they figure, whether within or without the Assembly, only as memories—memories that seem again to come to life so soon as the question is again only about the word "Republic," and as often as the revolutionary conflict threatens to sink down to the lowest level. In passing, I might observe that the journal which gave to this party its name, the "National," goes over to Socialism during. the following period.

Before we close this period, we must cast a look back upon the two powers, one of which destroys the other on December 2, 1851, while, from December 20, 1848, down to the departure of the constitutional assembly, they live in marital relations. We mean Louis Bonaparte, on the one hand, on the other, the party of the allied royalists, of Order, and of the large bourgeoisie.

At the inauguration of his presidency, Bonaparte forthwith framed a ministry out of the party of Order, at whose head he placed Odillon Barrot, be it noted, the old leader of the liberal wing of the parliamentary bourgeoisie. Mr. Barrot had finally hunted down a seat in the ministry, the spook of which had been pursuing him since 1830; and, what is more, he had the chairmanship in this ministry, although not, as he had imagined under Louis Philippe, the promoted leader of the parliamentary opposition, but with the commission to kill a parliament, and, moreover, as an ally of all his arch enemies, the Jesuits and the Legitimists. Finally he leads the bride home, but only after she has been prostituted. As to Bonaparte, he seemed to eclipse himself completely. The party of Order acted for him.

Immediately at the first session of the ministry the expedition to Rome was decided upon, which it was there agreed, was to be carried out behind the back of the National Assembly, and the funds for which, it was equally agreed, were to be wrung from the Assembly under false pretences. Thus the start was made with a swindle on the National Assembly, together with a secret conspiracy with the absolute foreign powers against the revolutionary Roman republic. In the same way, and with a similar maneuver, did Bonaparte prepare his stroke of December 2 against the royalist legislature and its constitutional republic. Let it not be forgotten that the same party, which, on December 20, 1848, constituted Bonaparte's

ministry, constituted also, on December 2, 1851,
the majority of the legislative National Assembly.

In August, the constitutive assembly decided
not to dissolve until it had prepared and promul-
gated a whole series of organic laws, intended
to supplement the Constitution. The party of
Order proposed to the assembly, through Representative Rateau, on January 6, 1819, to let the
organic laws go, and rather to order its own dissolution. Not the ministry alone, with Mr.
Odillon Barrot at its head, but all the royalist
members of the National Assembly were also at
this time hectoring to it that its dissolution was
necessary for the restoration of the public credit,
for the consolidation of order, to put an end to
the existing uncertain and provisional, and establish a definite state of things; they claimed that
its continued existence hindered the effectiveness
of the new Government, that it sought to prolong
its life out of pure malice, and that the country
was tired of it. Bonaparte took notice of all these
invectives hurled at the legislative power, he
learned them by heart, and, on December 21,
1851, he showed the parliamentary royalists that
he had learned from them. He repeated their
own slogans against themselves.

The Barrot ministry and the party of Order
went further. They called all over France for
petitions to the National Assembly in which that
body was politely requested to disappear. Thus
they led the people's unorganic masses to the
fray against the National Assembly, i. e., against
the constitutionally organized expression of the
people itself. They taught Bonaparte to appeal

from the parliamentary body to the people.
Finally, on January 29, 1849, the day arrived
when the constitutional assembly was to decide
about its own dissolution. On that day the body
found its building occupied by the military;
Changarnier, the General of the party of Order,
in whose hands was joined the supreme command
of both the National Guards and the regulars,
held that day a great military review, as though
a battle were imminent; and the coalized royalists
declared threateningly to the constitutional assembly that force would be applied if it did not
act willingly. It was willing, and chaffered only
for a very short respite. What else was the 29th
of January, 1849, than the "coup d'état" of December 2, 1851, only executed by the royalists
with Napoleon's aid against the republican National Assembly? These gentlemen did not notice, or did not want to notice, that Napoleon
utilized the 29th of January, 1849, to cause a
part of the troops to file before him in front of
the Tuileries, and that he seized with avidity this
very first open exercise of the military against
the parliamentary power in order to hint at
Caligula. The allied royalists saw only their own
Changarnier.

Another reason that particularly moved the
party of Order forcibly to shorten the term of
the constitutional assembly were the organic laws,
the laws that were to supplement the Constitution, as, for instance, the laws on education, on
religion, etc. The allied royalists had every interest in framing these laws themselves, and not
allowing them to be framed by the already suspicious republicans. Among these organic laws,

there was, however, one on the responsibility
of the President of the republic. In 1851 the
Legislature was just engaged in framing such a
law when Bonaparte forestalled that political
stroke by his own of December 2. What all
would not the coalized royalists have given in
their winter parliamentary campaign of 1851, had
they but found this "Responsibility law" ready
made, and framed at that, by the suspicious, the
vicious republican Assembly!

After, on January 29, 1849, the constitutive
assembly had itself broken its last weapon, the
Barrot ministry and the "Friends of Order" har-
rassed it to death, left nothing undone to humili-
tate it, and wrung from its weakness, despairing
of itself, laws that cost it the last vestige of re-
spect with the public. Bonaparte, occupied with
his own fixed Napoleonic idea, was audacious
enough openly to exploit this degradation of the
parliamentary power: When the National Assembly, on May 8, 1849, passed a vote of censure
upon the Ministry on account of the occupation
of Civita-Vecchia by Oudinot, and ordered that
the Roman expedition be brought back to its
alleged purpose, Bonaparte published that same
evening in the "Moniteur" a letter to Oudinot, in
which he congratulated him on his heroic feats,
and already, in contrast with the quill-pushing
parliamentarians, posed as the generous protector
of the Army. The royalists smiled at this. They
took him simply for their dupe. Finally, as Marrast, the President of the constitutional assembly, believed on a certain occasion the safety of
the body to be in danger, and, resting on the Constitution, made a requisition upon a Colonel, to-

gether with his regiment, the Colonel refused obedience, took refuge behind the "discipline," and referred Marrast to Changarnier, who scornfully sent him off with the remark that he did not like *"bayonettes intelligentes."*[3] In November, 1851, as the coalized royalists wanted to begin the decisive struggle with Bonaparte, they sought, by means of their notorious "Questors Bill," to enforce the principle of the right of the President of the National Assembly to issue direct requisitions for troops. One of their Generals, Leflo, supported the motion. In vain did Changarnier vote for it, or did Thiers render homage to the cautious wisdom of the late constitutional assembly. The Minister of War, St. Arnaud, answered him as Changarnier had answered Marrast—and he did so amidst the plaudits of the Mountain.

Thus did the party of Order itself, when as yet it was not the National Assembly, when as yet it was only a Ministry, brand the parliamentary regime. And yet this party objects vociferously when the 2d of December, 1851, banishes that regime from France!

We wish it a happy journey.

III.

On May 29, 1849, the legislative National Assembly convened. On December 2, 1851, it was broken up. This period embraces the term of life of the *Constitutional* or *Parliamentary Republic.*

---

[3] Intelligent bayonets.

In the first French revolution, upon the reign of the *Constitutionalists* succeeds that of the *Girondins;* and upon the reign of the *Girondins* follows that of the *Jacobins*. Each of these parties in succession rests upon its more advanced element. So soon as it has carried the revolution far enough not to be able to keep pace with, much less march ahead of it, it is shoved aside by its more daring allies, who stand behind it, and it is sent to the guillotine. Thus the revolution moves along an upward line.

Just the reverse in 1848. The proletarian party appears as an appendage to the small traders' or democratic party; it is betrayed by the latter and allowed to fall on April 16, May 15, and in the June days. In its turn, the democratic party leans upon the shoulders of the bourgeois republicans; barely do the bourgeois republicans believe themselves firmly in power, than they shake off these troublesome associates for the purpose of themselves leaning upon the shoulders of the party of Order. The party of Order draws in its shoulders, lets the bourgeois republicans tumble down heels over head, and throws itself upon the shoulders of the armed power. Finally, still of the mind that it is sustained by the shoulders of the armed power, the party of Order notices one fine morning that these shoulders have turned into bayonets. Each party kicks backward at those that are pushing forward, and leans forward upon those that are crowding backward; no wonder that, in this ludicrous posture, each loses its balance, and, after having cut the unavoidable grimaces, breaks down amid singular somersaults. Accordingly, the revolution moves along a downward line. It finds itself in this retreating motion before the last February-barricade is cleared away, and the first governmental authority of the revolution has been constituted.

The period we now have before us embraces the motliest jumble of crying contradictions: constitutionalists, who openly conspire against the Constitution; revolutionists, who admittedly are constitutional; a National Assembly that wishes to be omnipotent yet remains parliamentary; a Mountain, that finds its occupation in submission, and that parries its present defeats with prophecies of future victories; royalists, who constitute the "*patres conscripti*" of the republic, and are compelled by the situation to uphold abroad the hostile monarchic houses, whose adherents they are, while in France they support the republic that they hate; an Executive power that finds its strength in its very weakness, and its dignity in the contempt that it inspires; a republic, that is nothing else than the combined infamy of two monarchies—the Restoration and the July Monarchy—with an imperial label; unions, whose first clause is disunion; struggles, whose first law is indecision; in the name of peace, barren and hollow agitation; in the name of the revolution, solemn sermonizings on peace; passions without truth; truths without passion; heroes without heroism; history without events; development, whose only moving force seems to be the calendar, and tiresome by the constant reiteration of the same tensions and relaxes; contrasts, that seem to intensify themselves periodically, only in order to wear themselves off and collapse without a solution; pretentious efforts made for show, and bourgeois frights at the danger of the destruction of the world, simultaneous with the carrying on of the pettiest intrigues and the performance of court comedies by the world's saviours, who, in their "laisser aller," recall the Day of Judgment not so much as the days of the Fronde; the official collective genius of France brought to shame by the artful stupidity of a single individual; the collective will of the nation, as often as it speaks through the general suffrage, seeking its true expression in the prescriptive enemies of the public interests until it finally finds it in the arbitrary will of a filibuster. If ever a slice from history is drawn black upon black, it is this. Men and events appear as reversed "Schlemihls,"[1] as shadows, the bodies of which have been lost. The revolution itself paralyzes its own apostles, and equips only its adversaries with passionate violence. When the "Red Spectre," constantly conjured up and exorcised by the counter-revolutionists finally does appear, it does not appear with the Anarchist Phrygian cap on its head, but in the uniform of Order, in the *Red Breeches of the French Soldier.*

We saw that the Ministry, which Bonaparte installed on December 20, 1849, the day of his "Ascension," was a ministry of the party of Order, of the Legitimist and Orleanist coalition. The Barrot-Falloux Ministry had weathered the republican constitutive convention, whose term of life it had shortened with more or less violence, and found itself still at the helm. Chan-

---

[1] The hero in Chamisso's "Peter Schlemihl," who loses his own shadow.

garnier, the General of the allied royalists. continued to unite in his person the command-in-chief of the First Military Division and of the Parisian National Guard. Finally, the general elections had secured the large majority in the National Assembly to the party of Order. Here the Deputies and Peers of Louis Phillipe met a saintly crowd of Legitimists, for whose benefit numerous ballots of the nation had been converted into admission tickets to the political stage. The Bonapartist representatives were too thinly sowed to be able to build an independent parliamentary party. They appeared only as "mauvaise queue"[2] played upon the party of Order. Thus the party of Order was in possession of the Government, of the Army, and of the legislative body, in short, of the total power of the State, morally strengthened by the general elections, that caused their sovereignty to appear as the will of the people, and by the simultaneous victory of the counter-revolution on the whole continent of Europe.

Never did party open its campaign with larger means at its disposal and under more favorable auspices.

The shipwrecked pure republicans found themselves in the legislative National Assembly melted down to a clique of fifty men, with the African Generals Cavaignac, Lamorcière and Bedeau at its head. The great *Opposition* party was, however, formed by the Mountain. This parliamentary baptismal name was given to itself by the *Social Democratic party*. It disposed of more than two hundred votes out of the seven hundred and

[2] Practical joke.

fifty in the National Assembly, and, hence, was
at least just as powerful as any one of the three
factions of the party of Order. Its relative
minority to the total royalist colition seemed
counterbalanced by special circumstances. Not
only did the Departmental election returns show
that it had gained a considerable following
among the rural population, but, furthermore, it
numbered almost all the Paris Deputies in its
camp; the Army had, by the election of three
under-officers, made a confession of democratic
faith; and the leader of the Mountain, Ledru-
Rollin, had, in contrast to all the representatives
of the party of Order, been raised to the rank
of the "parliamentary nobility" by five Departments, who combined their suffrages upon him.
Accordingly, in view of the inevitable collisions
of the royalists among themselves, on the one
hand, and of the whole party of Order with
Bonaparte, on the other, the Mountain seemed
on May 29, 1849, to have before it all the elements of success. A fortnight later, it had lost
everything, its honor included.

Before we follow this parliamentary history
any further, a few observations are necessary,
in order to avoid certain common deceptions concerning the whole character of the epoch that
lies before us. According to the view of the
democrats, the issue, during the period of the
legislative National Assembly, was, the same as
during the period of the constitutive assembly,
simply the struggle between republicans and royalists; the movement itself was summed up by
them in the catch-word *Reaction*—night, in which
all cats are grey, and allows them to drawl out

their drowsy commonplaces. Indeed, at first
sight, the party of *Order* presents the appearance
of a tangle of royalist factions, that, not only intrigue against each other, each aiming to raise its
own Pretender to the throne, and exclude the
Pretender of the opposite party, but also are all
united in a common hatred for and common attacks against the "Republic." On its side, the
Mountain appears, in counter-distinction to the
royalist conspiracy, as the representative of the
"Republic." The party of *Order* seems constantly engaged in a "Reaction," which, neither
more nor less than in Prussia, is directed against
the press, the right of association and the like,
and is enforced by brutal police interventions on
the part of the bureaucracy, the police and the
public prosecutor—just as in Prussia; the *Mountain*, on the contrary, is engaged with equal
assiduity in parrying these attacks, and thus in
defending the "eternal rights of man"—as every
so-called people's party has more or less done
for the last hundred and fifty years. At a closer
inspection, however, of the situation and of the
parties, this superficial appearance, which veils
the *Class Struggle*, together with the peculiar
physiognomy of this period, vanishes wholly.

Legitimists and Orleanists constituted, as said
before, the two large factions of the party of
Order. What held these two factions to their
respective Pretenders, and inversely kept them
apart from each other, what else was it but the
lily and the tricolor, the House of Bourbon and
the House of Orleans, different shades of royalty? Under the Bourbons, *Large Landed Property* ruled together with its parsons and lackeys;

under the Orleanist, it was the high finance, large industry, large commerce, i. e., *Capital*, with its retinue of lawyers, professors and orators. The Legitimate kingdom was but the political expression for the hereditary rule of the landlords, as the July monarchy was but the political expression for the usurped rule of the bourgeois upstarts. What, accordingly, kept these two factions apart was no so-called set of principles, it was their material conditions for life—two different sorts of property—; it was the old antagonism of the City and the Country, the rivalry between Capital and Landed property. That simultaneously old recollections; personal animosities, fears and hopes; prejudices and illusions; sympathies and antipathies; convictions, faith and principles bound these factions to one House or the other, who denies it? Upon the several forms of property, upon the social conditions of existence, a whole superstructure is reared of various and peculiarly shaped feelings, illusions, habits of thought and conceptions of life. The whole class produces and shapes these out of its material foundation and out of the corresponding social conditions. The individual unit to whom they flow through tradition and education, may fancy that they constitute the true reasons for and premises of his conduct. Although Orleanists and Legitimists, each of these factions, sought to make itself and the other believe that what kept the two apart was the attachment of each to its respective royal House; nevertheless, facts proved later that it rather was their divided interest that forbade the union of the two royal Houses. As, in private life, the distinction is made between what a man thinks of himself and says, and that which he really is and does, so, all the more, must the phrases and notions of parties in historic struggles be distinguished from their real organism, and their real interests, their notions and their reality. Orleanists and Legitimists found themselves in the republic beside each other with equal claims. Each side wishing, in opposition to the other, to carry out the restoration of its own royal House, meant nothing else than that each of the two great *Interests* into which the bourgeoisie is divided—Land and Capital—sought to restore its own supremacy and the subordinacy of the other. We speak of two bourgeois interests because large landed property, despite its feudal coquetry and pride of race, has become completely bourgeois through the development of modern society. Thus did the Tories of England long fancy that they were enthusiastic for the Kingdom, the Church and the beauties of the old English Constitution, until the day of danger wrung from them the admission that their enthusiasm was only for *Ground-Rent*.

The coalized royalists carried on their intrigues against each other in the press, in Ems, in Clarmont—outside of the parliament. Behind the scenes, they don again their old Orleanist and Legitimist liveries, and conduct their old tourneys; on the public stage, however, in their public acts, as a great parliamentary party, they dispose of their respective royal Houses with mere courtesies, adjourn "in infinitum" the restoration of the monarchy. Their real business is trans-

acted as *Party of Order, i. e.,* under a *Social,* not
a *Political* title; as representatives of the bourgeois social system; not as knights of traveling
princesses, but as the bourgeois class against the
other classes; not as royalists against republicans.
Indeed, as party of Order they exercised a more
unlimited and harder dominion over the other
classes of society than ever before either under
the restoration or the July monarchy—a thing
possible only under the form of a parliamentary
republic, because under this form alone could
the two large divisions of the French bourgeoisie be united; in other words, only under
this form could they place on the order of busi-
nes the sovereignty of their class, in lieu of the
régime of a privileged faction of the same. If,
this nothwithstanding, they are seen as the
party of Order to insult the republic and express
their antipathy for it, it happened not out of
royalist traditions only: Instinct taught them that
while, indeed, the republic completes their authority, it at the same time undermined their
social foundation, in that, without intermediary,
without the mask of the crown, without being
able to turn aside the national interest by means
of its subordinate struggles among its own conflicting elements and with the crown, the republic
is compelled to stand up sharp against the sub-
jugated classes, and wrestle with them. It was
a sense of weakness that caused them to recoil
before the unqualified demands of their own class
rule, and to retreat to the less complete, less developed, and, for that very reason, less dangerous
forms of the same. As often, on the contrary,
as the allied royalists come into conflict with the

Pretender who stands before them—with Bonaparte—, as often as they believe their parliamentary omnipotence to be endangered by the Executive, in other words, as often as they must trot out the political title of their authority, they step up as *Republicans,* not as *Royalists*—and this is done from the Orleanist Thiers, who warns the National Assembly that the republic divides them least, down to Legitimist Berryer, who, on December 2, 1851, the scarf of the tricolor around him, harangues the people assembled before the Mayor's building of the Tenth Arrondissement, as a tribune in the name of the Republic; the echo, however, derisively answering back to him: "Henry V.! Henry V.!"'

However, against the allied bourgeois, a coalition was made between the small traders and the workingmen—the so-called *Social Democratic* party. The small traders found themselves ill rewarded after the June days of 1848; they saw their material interests endangered, and the democratic guarantees, that were to uphold their interests, made doubtful. Hence, they drew closer to the workingmen. On the other hand, their parliamentary representatives—the *Mountain*—, after being shoved aside during the dictatorship of the bourgeois republicans, had, during the last half of the term of the constitutive convention, regained their lost popularity through the struggle with Bonaparte and the royalist ministers. They had made an alliance with the Socialist leaders. During February, 1849, reconciliation banquets were held. A common pro-

* The candidate of the Bourbons, or Legitimists, for the throne.

gram was drafted, joint election committees were empaneled, and fusion candidates were set up. The revolutionary point was thereby broken off from the social demands of the proletariat, and a democratic turn given to them; while, from the democratic claims of the small traders' class, the mere political form was rubbed off and the Socialist point was pushed forward. Thus came the *Social Democracy* about. The new *Mountain*, the result of this combination, contained, with the exception of some figures from the working class and some Socialist sectarians, the identical elements of the old Mountain, only numerically stronger. In the course of events it had, however, changed, together with the class that it represented. The peculiar character of the Social Democracy is summed up in this: that democratic-republican institutions are demanded as the means, not to remove the two extremes—Capital and Wage-slavery—, but in order to weaken their antagonism and transform them into a harmonious whole. However different the methods may be that are proposed for the accomplishment of this object, however much the object itself may be festooned with more or less revolutionary fancies, the substance remains the same. This substance is the transformation of society upon democratic lines, but a transformation within the boundaries of the small traders' class. No one must run away with the narrow notion that the small traders' class means on principle to enforce a selfish class interest. It believes rather that the special conditions for its own emancipation are the general conditions under which alone modern society can be saved and the class struggle

avoided. Likewise must we avoid running away
with the notion that the Democratic Representatives are all "shopkeepers," or enthuse for these.
They may—by educaton and individual standing
—be as distant from them as heaven is from
earth. That which makes them representatives
of the small traders' class is that they do not in-
tellectually leap the bounds which that class itself
does not leap in practical life; that, consequently,
they are theoretically driven to the same problems and solutions, to which material interests
and social standing practically drive the latter.
Such, in fact, is at all times the relation of the
"political" and the "literary" representatives of a
class to the class they represent.

After the foregoing explanations, it goes without saying that, while the Mountain is constantly
wrestling for the republic and the so-called
"rights of man," neither the republic nor the
"rights of man" is its real goal, as little as an
army, whose weapons it is sought to deprive it
of and that defends itself, steps on the field of
battle simply in order to remain in possession of
its implements of warfare.

The party of Order provoked the Mountain immediately upon the convening of the assembly
The bourgeoisie now felt the necessity of dispos-
ing of the democratic small traders' class, just
as a year before it had understood the necessity
of putting an end to the revolutionary proletariat.

But the position of the foe had changed. The
strength of the proletarian party was on the
streets; that of the small traders' class was in the
National Assembly itself. The point was, accordingly, to wheedle them out of the National

Assembly into the street, and to have them break their parliamentary power themselves, before time and opportunity could consolidate them. The Mountain jumped with loose reins into the trap.

The bombardment of Rome by the French troops was the bait thrown at the Mountain. It violated Article V. of the Constitution, which forbade the French republic to use its forces against the liberties of other nations; besides, Article IV. forbade all declaration of war by the Executive without the consent of the National Assembly; furthermore, the constitutive assembly had censured the Roman expedition by its resolution of May 8. Upon these grounds, Ledru-Rollin submitted on June 11, 1849, a motion impeaching Bonaparte and his Ministers. Instigated by the wasp-stings of Thiers, he even allowed himself to be carried away to the point of threatening to defend the Constitution by all means, even arms in hand. The Mountain rose as one man, and repeated the challenge. On June 12, the National Assembly rejected the notion to impeach, and the Mountain left the parliament. The events of June 13 are known: the proclamation by a part of the Mountain pronouncing Napoleon and his Ministers "outside the pale of the Constitution"; the street parades of the democratic National Guards, who, unarmed as they were, flew apart at contact with the troops of Changarnier; etc., etc. Part of the Mountain fled abroad, another part was assigned to the High Court of Bourges, and a parliamentary regulation placed the rest under the school-master supervision of the President

of the National Assembly. Paris was again
put under a state of siege; and the democratic portion of the National Guards was disbanded. Thus the influence of the Mountain in
parliament was broken, together with the power
of the small traders' class in Paris.

Lyons, where the 13th of June had given the
signal to a bloody labor uprising, was, together
with the five surrounding Departments, likewise
pronounced in state of siege, a condition that continues down to this moment.[4]

The bulk of the Mountain had left its vanguard in the lurch by refusing their signatures
to the proclamation; the press had deserted: only
two papers dared to publish the pronunciamento;
the small traders had betrayed their Representatives: the National Guards stayed away, or,
where they did turn up, hindered the raising of
barricades; the Representatives had duped the
small traders: nowhere were the alleged affiliated
members from the Army to be seen; finally, instead of gathering strength from them, the democratic party had infected the proletariat with its
own weakness, and, as usual with democratic
feats, the leaders had the satisfaction of charging "their people" with desertion, and the people
had the satisfaction of charging their leaders
with fraud.

Seldom was an act announced with greater
noise than the campaign contemplated by the
Mountain; seldom was an event trumpeted ahead
with more certainty and longer beforehand than
the "inevitable victory of the democracy." This
is evident: the democrats believe in the trom-

---

[4] January, 1852.

bones before whose blasts the walls of Jericho fall together; as often as they stand before the walls of despotism, they seek to imitate the miracle. If the Mountain wished to win in parliament, it should not appeal to arms; if it called to arms in parliament, it should not conduct itself parliamentarily on the street; if the friendly demonstration was meant seriously, it was silly not to foresee that it would meet with a warlike reception; if it was intended for actual war, it was rather original to lay aside the weapons with which war had to be conducted. But the revolutionary threats of the middle class and of their democratic representatives are mere attempts to frighten an adversary; when they have run themselves into a blind alley, when they have sufficiently compromised themselves and are compelled to execute their threats, the thing is done in a hesitating manner that avoids nothing so much as the means to the end, and catches at pretexts to succumb. The bray of the overture, that announces the fray, is lost in a timid growl so soon as this is to start; the actors cease to take themselves seriously, and the performance falls flat like an inflated balloon that is pricked with a needle.

No party exaggerates to itself the means at its disposal more than the democratic, none deceives itself with greater heedlessness on the situation. A part of the Army voted for it, thereupon the Mountain is of the opinion that the Army would revolt in its favor. And by what occasion? By an occasion, that, from the standpoint of the troops, meant nothing else than that the revolutionary soldiers should take the part

of the soldiers of Rome against French soldiers.
On the other hand, the memory of June, 1848,
was still too fresh not to keep alive a deep aver-
sion on the part of the proletariat towards the
National Guard, and a strong feeling of mistrust
on the part of the leaders of the secret societies
for the democratic leaders. In order to balance
these differences, great common interests at stake
were needed. The violation of an abstract constitutional paragraph could not supply such interests. Had not the constitution been repeatedly
violated, according to the assurances of the democrats themselves? Had not the most popular papers branded them as a counter-revolutionary
artifice? But the democrat—by reason of his
representing the middle class, that is to say, a
Transition Class, in which the interests of two
other classes are mutually dulled—, imagines himself above all class contrast. The democrats
grant that opposed to them stands a privileged
class, but they, together with the whole remain-
ing mass of the nation, constitute the "PEO-
PLE." What they represent is the "people's
rights"; their interests are the "people's interests." Hence, they do not consider that, at an
impending struggle, they need to examine the
interests and attitude of the different classes.
They need not too seriously weigh their own
means. All they have to do is to give the signal
in order to have the "people" fall upon the "op-
pressors" with all its inexhaustible resources.
If, thereupon, in the execution, their interests
turn out to be uninteresting, and their power to
be impotence, it is ascribed either to depraved
sophists, who split up the "undivisible people"

into several hostile camps; or to the army being too far brutalized and blinded to appreciate the pure aims of the democracy as its own best; or to some detail in the execution that wrecks the whole plan; or, finally, to an unforeseen accident that spoiled the game this time. At all events, the democrat comes out of the disgraceful defeat as immaculate as he went innocently into it, and with the refreshed conviction that he must win; not that he himself and his party must give up their old standpoint, but that, on the contrary conditions must come to his aid.

For all this, one must not picture to himself the decimated, broken, and, by the new parliamentary regulation, humbled Mountain altogether too unhappy. If June 13 removed its leaders, it on the other hand, made room for new ones of inferior capacity, who are flattered by their new position. If their impotence in parliament could no longer be doubted, they were now justified to limit their activity to outbursts of moral indignation. If the party of Order pretended to see in them, as the last official representatives of the revolution, all the horrors of anarchy incarnated, they were free to appear all the more flat and modest in reality. Over June 13 they consoled themselves with the profound expression: "If they but dare to assail universal suffrage . . . then . . . then we will show who we are!" Nous verrons.[5]

As to the "Mountaineers," who had fled abroad, it suffices here to say that Ledru-Rollin— he having accomplished the feat of hopelessly ruining, in barely a fortnight, the powerful party

---

[5] We shall see.

at whose head he stood—, found himself called upon to build up a French government "in partibus;" that his figure, at a distance, removed from the field of action, seemed to gain in size in the measure that the level of the revolution sank and the official prominences of official France became more and more dwarfish; that he could figure as republican Pretender for 1852, and periodically issued to the Wallachians and other peoples circulars in which "despot of the continent" is threatened with the feats that he and his allies had in contemplation. Was Proudhon wholly wrong when he cried out to these gentlemen: "Vous n'êtes que des blaqueurs"?[6]

The party of Order had, on June 13, not only broken up the Mountain, it had also established the *Subordination of the Constitution to the Majority Decisions of the National Assembly.* So, indeed, did the republic understand it, to-wit, that the bourgeois ruled here in parliamentary form, without, as in the monarchy, finding a check in the veto of the Executive power, or the liability of parliament to dissolution. It was a "parliamentary republic," as Thiers styled it. But if, on June 13, the bourgeoisie secured its omnipotence within the parliament building, did it not also strike the parliament itself, as against the Executive and the people, with incurable weakness by excluding its most popular part? By giving up numerous Deputies, without further ceremony to the mercies of the public prosecutor, it abolished its own parliamentary inviolability. The humiliating regulation, that it subjected the Mountain to, raised the President of the republic

_____
[6] You are nothing but fakirs.

in the same measure that it lowered the individua
Representatives of the people. By branding ai
insurrection in defense of the Constitution a
anarchy, and as a deed looking to the overthrov
of society, it interdicted to itself all appeal to
insurrection whenever the Executive should vio
late the Constitution against it. And, indeed, the
irony of history wills it that the very General
who by order of Bonaparte bombarded Rome, and
thus gave the immediate occasion to the constitu
tional riot of June 13, that *Oudinot*, on Decem
ber 2, 1851, is the one imploringly and vainly
to be offered to the people by the party of Orde
as the General of the Constitution. Another here
of June 13, Vieyra, who earned praise from the
tribune of the National Assembly for the brutali
ties that he had committed in the democratic
newspaper offices at the head of a gang of Na
tional Guards in the hire of the high finance—
this identical Vieyra was initiated in the conspi
racy of Bonaparte, and contributed materially ii
cutting off all protection that could come to the
National Assembly, in the hour of its agony
from the side of the National Guard.

June 13 had still another meaning. The Moun
tain had wanted to place Bonaparte undei
charges. Their defeat was, accordingly, a direc
victory of Bonaparte; it was his personal triumpl
over his democratic enemies. The party of Ordei
fought for the victory, Bonaparte needed only
to pocket it. He did so. On June 14, a procla
mation was to be read on the walls of Paris
wherein the President, as it were, without his
connivance, against his will, driven by the mere
force of circumstances, steps forward from his

loisterly seclusion like misjudged virtue, com-
lains of the calumnies of his antagonists, and,
while seeming to identify his own person with
the cause of order, rather identifies the cause of
rder with his own person. Besides this, the
National Assembly had subsequently approved the
xpedition against Rome; Bonaparte, however,
ad taken the initiative in the affair. After he
ad led the High Priest Samuel back into the
Vatican, he could hope as King David to occupy
the Tuileries. He had won the parson-interests
ver to himself.

The riot of June 13 limited itself, as we have
een, to a peaceful street procession. There were,
onsequently, no laurels to be won from it. Nev-
rtheless, in these days, poor in heroes and events,
the party of Order converted this bloodless bat-
e into a second Austerlitz. Tribune and press
auded the army as the power of order against
the popular multitude, and the impotence of an-
rchy; and Changarnier as the "bulwark of so-
ety"—a mystification that he finally believed
in himself. Underhand, however, the corps that
eemed doubtful were removed from Paris; the
egiments whose suffrage had turned out most
emocratic were banished from France to Al-
iers; the restless heads among the troops were
onsigned to penal quarters; finally, the shut-
ng out of the press from the barracks, and of
the barracks from contact with the citizens was
systematically carried out.

We stand here at the critical turning point in
the history of the French National Guard. In
830, it had decided the downfall of the restora-
on. Under Louis Philippe, every riot failed, at

which the National Guard stood on the side of the troops. When, in the February days of 1848, it showed itself passive against the uprising and doubtful toward Louis Philippe himself, he gave himself up for lost. Thus the conviction cast root that a revolution could not win without, nor the Army against, the National Guard. This was the superstitious faith of the Army in bourgeois omnipotence. The June days of 1848, when the whole National Guard, jointly with the regular troops, threw down the insurrection, had confirmed the superstition. After the inauguration of Bonaparte's administration, the position of the National Guard sank somewhat through the unconstitutional joining of their command with the command of the First Military Division in the person of Changarnier.

As the command of the National Guard appeared here merely an attribute of the military commander-in-chief, so did the Guard itself appear only as an appendage of the regular troops. Finally, on June 13, the National Guard was broken up, not through its partial dissolution only, that from that date forward was periodically repeated at all points of France, leaving only wrecks of its former self behind. The demonstration of June 13 was, above all, a demonstration of the National Guards. True, they had not carried their arms, but they had carried their uniforms against the Army—and the talisman lay just in these uniforms. The Army then learned that this uniform was but a woolen rag, like any other. The spell was broken. In the June days of 1848, bourgeoisie and small traders were united as National Guard with the Army against the proletariat; on June 13, 1849, the bourgeoisie had the small-traders' National Guard broken up; on December 2, 1851, the National Guard of the bourgeoisie itself vanished, and Bonaparte attested the fact when he subsequently signed the decree for its disbandment. Thus the bourgeoisie had itself broken its last weapon against the army, from the moment when the small traders' class no longer stood as a vassal behind, but as a rebel before it; indeed, it was bound to do so, as it was bound to destroy with its own hand all its means of defence against absolutism, so soon as itself was absolute.

In the meantime, the party of Order celebrated the recovery of a power that seemed lost in 1848 only in order that, freed from its trammels in 1849, it be found again through invectives against the republic and the Constitution; through the malediction of all future, present and past revolutions, that one included which its own leaders had made; and, finally, in laws by which the press was gagged, the right of association destroyed, and the stage of siege regulated as an organic institution. The National Assembly then adjourned from the middle of August to the middle of October, after it had appointed a Permanent Committee for the period of its absence. During these vacations, the Legitimists intrigued with Ems; the Orleanists with Claremont; Bonaparte through princely excursions; the Departmental Councilmen in conferences over the revision of the Constitution:— occurrences, all of which recurred regularly at the periodical vacations of the National Assembly, and upon which I shall not enter until they have matured into events. Be it here only observed that the National Assembly was impolitic in vanishing from the stage for long intervals, and leaving in view, at the head of the republic, only one, however sorry, figure—Louis Bonaparte's—, while, to the public scandal, the party of Order broke up into its own royalist component parts, that pursued their conflicting aspirations after the restoration. As often as, during these vacations, the confusing noise of the parliament was hushed, and its body was dissolved in the nation, it was unmistakably shown that only one thing was still wanting to complete the true figure of the republic: to make the vacation of the National Assembly permanent, and substitute its inscription—"Liberty, Equality, Fraternity"—by the unequivocal words, "Infantry, Cavalry, Artillery!"

IV.

The National Assembly reconvened in the middle of October. On November 1, Bonaparte surprised it with a message, in which he announced the dismissal of the Barrot-Falloux Ministry, and the framing of a new. Never have lackeys been chased from service with less ceremony than Bonaparte did his ministers. The kicks, that were eventually destined for the National Assembly, Barrot & Company received in the meantime.

The Barrot Ministry was, as we have seen, composed of Legitimists and Orleanists; it was a Ministry of the party of Order. Bonaparte needed that Ministry in order to dissolve the republican constituent assembly, to effect the expedition against Rome, and to break up the democratic party. He had seemingly eclipsed himself behind this Ministry, yielded the reins to the hands of the party of Order, and assumed the modest mask, which, under Louis Philippe, had been worn by the responsible overseer of the newspapers—the mask of "homme de paille."[1] Now he threw off the mask, it being no longer the light curtain behind which he could conceal, but the Iron Mask, which prevented him from revealing his own physiognomy. He had instituted the Barrot Ministry in order to break up the republican National Assembly in the name of the party of Order; he now dismissed it in order to declare his own name independent of the parliament of the party of Order.

There was no want of plausible pretexts for this dismissal. The Barrot Ministry had neglected even the forms of decency that would have allowed the president of the republic to appear as a power along with the National Assembly. For instance, during the vacation of the National Assembly, Bonaparte published a letter to Edgar Ney, in which he seemed to disapprove the liberal attitude of the Pope, just as, in opposition to the constitutive assembly, he had published a letter, in which he praised Oudinot for his attack upon the Roman republic; when the National Assembly came to vote on the budget for the Roman expedition, Victor Hugo, out of pretended liberalism, brought up that letter for discussion; the party of Order drowned this notion of Bonaparte's under exclamations of contempt

---

[1] Man of straw.

and incredulity as though notions of Bonaparte could not possibly have any political weight;—and none of the Ministers took up the gauntlet for him. On another occasion, Barrot, with his well-known hollow pathos, dropped, from the speakers' tribune in the Assembly, words of indignation upon the 'abominable machinations," which, according to him, went on in the immediate vicinity of the President. Finally, while the Ministry obtained from the National Assembly a widow's pension for the Duchess of Orleans, it denied every motion to raise the Presidential civil list;—and, in Bonaparte, be it always remembered, the Imperial Pretender was so closely blended with the impecunious adventurer, that the great idea of his being destined to restore the Empire was ever supplemented by that other, to-wit, that the French people was destined to pay his debts.

The Barrot-Falloux Ministry was the first and last parliamentary Ministry that Bonaparte called into life. Its dismissal marks, accordingly, a decisive period. With the Ministry, the party of Order lost, never to regain, an indispensable post to the maintenance of the parliamentary régime,—the handle to the Executive power. It is readily understood that, in a country like France, where the Executive disposes over an army of more than half a million office-holders, and, consequently, keeps permanently a large mass of interests and existences in the completest dependence upon itself; where the Government surrounds, controls, regulates, supervises and guards society, from its mightiest acts of national life, down to its most insignificant mo-

tions; from its common life, down to the private
life of each individual; where, due to such extraordinary centralization, this body of parasites
acquires a ubiquity and omniscience, a quickened
capacity for motion and rapidity that finds an
analogon only in the helpless lack of self-reliance,
in the unstrung weakness of the body social itself;
—that in such a country the National Assembly
lost, with the control of the ministerial posts, all
real influence, unless it simultaneously simplified
the administration; if possible, reduced the army
of office-holders; and, finally, allowed society and
public opinion to establish its own organs, independent of government censorship. But the
Material Interest of the French bourgeoisie is
most intimately bound up in maintenance of just
such a large and extensively ramified governmental machine. There the bourgeoisie provides for its own superfluous membership; and
supplies, in the shape of government salaries,
what it can not pocket in the form of profit, interest, rent and fees. On the other hand, its
Political Interests daily compel it to increase the
power of repression, *i. e.,* the means and the per-
sonnel of the government; it is at the same time
forced to conduct an uninterrupted warfare
against public opinion, and, full of suspicion, to
hamstring and lame the independent organs of
society—whenever it does not succeed in ampu-
tating them wholly. Thus the bourgeoisie of
France was forced by its own class attitude, on
the one hand, to destroy the conditions for all
parliamentary power, its own included, and, on
the other, to render irresistible the Executive
power that stood hostile to it.

The new Ministry was called the d'Hautpoul Ministry. Not that General d'Hautpoul had gained the rank of Ministerial President. Along with Barrot, Bonaparte abolished this dignity, which, it must be granted, condemned the President of the republic to the legal nothingness of a constitutional kind, of a constitutional king at that, without throne and crown, without sceptre and without sword, without irresponsibility, without the imperishable possession of the highest dignity in the State, and, what was most untoward of all—without a civil list. The d'Hautpoul Ministry numbered only one man of parliamentary reputation, the Jew Fould, one of the most notorious members of the high finance. To him fell the portfolio of finance. Turn to the Paris stock quotations, and it will be found that from November 1, 1849, French stocks fall and rise with the falling and rising of the Bonapartist shares. While Bonaparte had thus found his ally in the Bourse, he at the same time took possession of the Police through the appointment of Carlier as Prefect of Police.

But the consequences of the change of Ministry could reveal themselves only in the course of events. So far, Bonaparte had taken only one step forward, to be all the more glaringly driven back. Upon his harsh message, followed the most servile declarations of submissiveness to the National Assembly. As often as the Ministers made timid attempts to introduce his own personal hobbies as bills, they themselves seemed unwilling and compelled only by their position to run the comic errands, of whose futility they were convinced in advance. As often as Bonaparte blabbed out his plans behind the backs of his Ministers, and sported his "idées napoléoniennes,"[2] his own Ministers disavowed him from the speakers' tribune in the National Assembly. His aspirations after usurpation seemed to become audible only to the end that the ironical laughter of his adversaries should not die out. He deported himself like an unappreciated genius, whom the world takes for a simpleton. Never did he enjoy in fuller measure the contempt of all classes than at this period. Never did the bourgeoisie rule more absolutely; never did it more boastfully display the insignia of sovereignty.

It is not here my purpose to write the history of its legislative activity, which is summed up in two laws passed during this period: the law reestablishing the duty on wine, and the laws on education, to suppress infidelity. While the drinking of wine was made difficult to the Frenchmen, all the more bounteously was the water of pure life poured out to them. Although in the law on the duty on wine the bourgeoisie declares the old hated French tariff system to be inviolable, it sought, by means of the laws on education, to secure the old good will of the masses that made the former bearable. One wonders to see the Orleanists, the liberal bourgeois, these old apostles of Voltarianism and of eclectic philosophy, entrusting the supervision of the French intellect to their hereditary enemies, the Jesuits. But, while Orleanists and Legitimists could part company on the question of the Pretender to the crown, they understood full well that their joint reign dictated the joining of the means of op-

---

[2] Napoleonic ideas.

pression of two distinct epochs; that the means of
subjugation of the July monarchy had to be supplemented with and strengthened by the means
of subjugation of the restoration.

The farmers, deceived in all their expectations,
more than ever ground down by the law scale
of the price of corn, on the one hand, and, on
the other, by the growing load of taxation and
mortgages, began to stir in the Departments.
They were answered by the systematic baiting
of the school masters, whom the Government
subjected to the clergy; by the systematic baiting
of the Mayors, whom it subjected to the Prefects;
and by a system of espionage to which all were
subjected. In Paris and the large towns, the
reaction itself carries the physiognomy of its
own epoch; it irritates more than it cows; in the
country, it becomes low, mean, petty, tiresome,
vexatious,—in a word, it becomes "gensdarme."
It is easily understood how three years of the
gensdarme régime, sanctified by the régime of
the clergyman, was bound to demoralize unripe
masses.

Whatever the mass of passion and declamation,
that the party of Order expended from the speakers' tribune in the National Assembly against the
minority, its speech remained monosyllabic, like
that of the Christian, whose speech was to be
"Aye, aye; nay, nay." It was monosyllabic,
whether from the tribune or the press; dull as a
conundrum, whose solution is known beforehand. Whether the question was the right of pe-
tition or the duty on wine, the liberty of the
press or free trade, clubs or municipal laws, protection of individual freedom or the regulation of

national economy, the slogan returns ever again, the theme is monotonously the same, the verdict is ever ready and unchanged: *Socialism!* Even bourgeois liberalism is pronounced socialistic; socialistic, alike, is pronounced popular education; and, likewise, socialistic national financial reform. It was socialistic to build a railroad where already a canal was; and it was socialistic to defend oneself with a stick when attacked with a sword.

This was not a mere form of speech, a fashion, nor yet party tactics. The bourgeoisie perceives correctly that all the weapons, which it forged against feudalism, turn their edges against itself; that all the means of education, which it brought forth, rebel against its own civiliaztion; that all the gods, which it made, have fallen away from it. It understands that all its so-called citizens' rights and progressive organs assail and menace its class rule, both in its social foundation and its political superstructure—consequently, have become "socialistic." It justly scents in this menace and assault the secret of *Socialism*, whose meaning and tendency it estimates more correctly than the spurious, so-called Socialism, is capable of estimating itself, and which, consequently, is unable to understand how it is that the bourgeoisie obdurately shuts up its ears to it, alike whether it sentimentally whines about the sufferings of humanity; or announces in Christian style the millennium and universal brotherhood; or twaddles humanistically about the soul, culture and freedom; or doctrinally matches out a system of harmony and wellbeing for all classes. What, however, the bourgeoisie does not understand is the consequence that its own parliamentary régime, its own political reign, is also of necessity bound to fall under the general ban of "socialistic." So long as the rule of the bourgeoisie is not fully organized, has not acquired its purely political character, the contrast with the other classes cannot come into view in all its sharpness; and, where it does come into view, it cannot take that dangerous turn that converts every conflict with the Government into a conflict with Capital. When, however, the French bourgeoisie began to realize in every pulsation of society a menace to "peace," how could it, at the head of society, pretend to uphold the régime of unrest, its own régime, the parliamentary régime, which, according to the expression of one of its own orators, lives in struggle, and through struggle? The parliamentary régime lives on discussion,—how can it forbid discussion? Every single interest, every single social institution is there converted into general thoughts, is treated as a thought,—how could any interest or institution claim to be above thought, and impose itself as an article of faith? The orators' conflict in the tribune calls forth the conflict of the rowdies in the press; the debating club in parliament is necessarily supplemented by debating clubs in the salons and the bar-rooms; the representatives, who are constantly appealing to popular opinion, justify popular opinion in expressing its real opinion in petitions. The parliamentary régime leaves everything to the decision of majorities,—how can the large majorities beyond parliament be expected not to wish to decide? If, from above, they hear the fiddle screeching, what else is to be expected than that those below should dance?

Accordingly, by now persecuting as *Socialist* what formerly it had celebrated as *Liberal,* the bourgeoisie admits that its own interest orders it to raise itself above the danger of self government; that, in order to restore rest to the land, it own bourgeois parliament must, before all, be brought to rest; that, in order to preserve its social power unhurt, its political power must be broken; that the private bourgeois can continue to exploit the other classes and rejoice in "property," "family," "religion" and "order" only under the condition that his own class be condemned to the same political nullity of the other classes; that, in order to save their purse, the crown must be knocked off their heads, and the sword, that was to shield them, must at the same time be hung over their heads as a sword of Damocles.

In the domain of general bourgeois interests, the National Assembly proved itself so barren, that, for instance, the discussion over the Paris-Avignon railroad, opened in the winter of 1850, was not yet ripe for a vote on December 2, 1851. Wherever it did not oppress or was reactionary, the bourgeoisie was smitten with incurable barrenness.

While Bonaparte's Ministry either sought to take the initiative of laws in the spirit of the party of Order, or even exaggerated their severity in their enforcement and administration, he, on his part, sought to win popularity by means of childishly silly propositions, to exhibit the contrast between himself and the National Assembly, and to hint at a secret plan, held in reserve and only through circumstances temporarily prevented from disclosing its hidden treasures to the French people. Of this nature was the proposition to decree a daily extra pay of four sous to the under-officers; so, likewise, the proposition for a "word of honor" loan bank for working-men. To have money given and money borrowed—that was the perspective that he hoped to cajole the masses with. Presents and loans—to that was limited the financial wisdom of the slums, the high as well as the low; to that were limited the springs which Bonaparte knew how to set in motion. Never did Pretender speculate more dully upon the dullness of the masses.

Again and again did the National Assembly fly into a passion at these unmistakable attempts to win popularity at its expense, and at the growing danger that this adventurer, lashed on by debts and unrestrained by reputation, might venture upon some desperate act. The strained relations between the party of Order and the President had taken on a threatening aspect, when an unforeseen event threw him back, rueful into its arms. We mean the supplementary elections of March, 1850. These elections took place to fill the vacancies created in the National Assembly, after June 13, by imprisonment and exile. Paris elected only Social-Democratic candidates; it even united the largest vote upon one of the insurgents of June, 1818,—Deflotte. In this way the small traders' world of Paris, now allied with the proletariat, revenged itself for the defeat of June 13, 1849. It seemed to have disappeared from the field of battle at the hour of danger only to step on it again at a more favorable opportunity, with increased forces for the fray, and with a bolder war cry. A circumstance seemed to heighten the danger of this electoral victory. The Army voted in Paris for a June insurgent against Lahitte, a Minister of Bonaparte's, and, in the Departments, mostly for the candidates of the Mountain, who, there also, although not as decisively as in Paris, maintained the upper hand over their adversaries.

Bonaparte suddenly saw himself again face to face with the revolution. As on January 29, 1849, as on June 13, 1849, on May 10, 1850, he vanished again behind the party of Order. He bent low; he timidly apologized; he offered to appoint any Ministry whatever at the behest of the parliamentary majority; he even implored the Orleanist and Legitimist party leaders—the Thiers, Berryers, Broglies, Molés, in short, the so-called burgraves—to take hold of the helm of State in person. The party of Order did not know how to utilize this opportunity, that was never to return. Instead of boldly taking possession of the proffered power, it did not even force Bonaparte to restore the Ministry, dismissed on November 1; it contented itself with humiliating him with its pardon, and with affiliating Mr. Baroche to the d'Hautpoul Ministry. This Baroche had, as Public Prosecutor, stormed before the High Court at Bourges, once against the revolutionists of May 15, another time against the Democrats of June 13, both times on the charge of "attentats" against the National Assembly. None of Bonaparte's Ministers contributed later more towards the degradation of the National Assembly; and, after December 2, 1851, we meet him again as the comfortably stalled and dearly paid Vice-President of the Senate. He had spat into the soup of the revolutionists for Bonaparte to eat it.

On its part, the Social Democratic party seemed only to look for pretexts in order to make its own victory doubtful, and to dull its edge. Vidal, one of the newly elected Paris representatives, was returned for Strassburg also. He was induced to decline the seat for Paris and accept the one for Strassburg. Thus, instead of giving a definite character to their victory at the hustings, and thereby compelling the party of Order forthwith to contest it in parliament; instead of thus driving the foe to battle at the season of popular enthusiasm and of a favorable temper in the Army, the democratic party tired out Paris with a new campaign during the months of March and April; it allowed the excited popular passions to wear themselves out in this second provisional electoral play; it allowed the revolutionary vigor to satiate itself with constitutional successes, and lose its breath in petty intrigues, hollow declamation and sham moves; it gave the bourgeoisie time to collect itself and make its preparations; finally, it allowed the significance of the March elections to find a sentimentally weakening commentary at the subsequent April election in the victory of Eugene Sue. In one word, it turned the 10th of March into an April Fool.

The parliamentary majority perceived the weakness of its adversary. Its seventeen burgraves—Bonaparte had left to it the direction of and responsibility for the attack—, framed a new election law, the moving of which was entrusted to Mr. Faucher, who had applied for the honor. On May 8, he introduced the new law whereby universal suffrage was abolished; a three years' residence in the election district imposed as a condition for voting; and, finally, the proof of this residence made dependent, for the working-man, upon the testimony of his employer.

As revolutionarily as the democrats had agitated and stormed during the constitutional struggles, so constitutionally did they, now, when it was imperative to attest, arms in hand, the earnestness of their late electoral victories, preach order, "majestic calmness," lawful conduct, i. e., blind submission to the will of the counter-revolution, which revealed itself as law. During the debate, the Mountain put the party of Order to shame by maintaining the passionless attitude of the law-abiding burger, who upholds the principle of law against revolutionary passions; and by twitting the party of Order with the fearful reproach of proceeding in a revolutionary manner. Even the newly elected deputies took pains to prove by their decent and thoughtful deportment what an act of misjudgment it was to decry them as anarchists, or explain their election as a victory of the revolution. The new election law was passed on May 31. The Mountain contented itself with smuggling a protest into the pockets of the President of the Assembly. To the election law followed a new press law, whereby the revolutionary press was completely done away with. It had deserved its fate. The "National" and the "Presse," two bourgeois organs, re-

mained after this deluge the extreme outposts of
the revolution.

We have seen how, during March and April,
the democratic leaders did everything to involve
the people of Paris in a sham battle, and how,
after May 8, they did everything to keep it away
from a real battle. We may not here forget that
the year 1850 was one of the most brilliant years
of industrial and commercial prosperity; consequently, that the Parisian proletariat was completely employed. But the election law of May
31, 1850, excluded them from all participation
in political power; it cut the field of battle itself
from under them; it threw the workingmen
back into the state of pariahs, which they had
occupied before the February revolution. In
allowing themselves, in sight of such an occurrence, to be led by the democrats, and in for-
getting the revolutionary interests of their class
through temporary comfort, the workingmen ab-
dicated the honor of being a conquering power;
they submitted to their fate; they proved that the
defeat of June, 1848, had incapacitated them from
resistance for many a year to come; finally, that
the historic process must again, for the time being, proceed over their heads. As to the small
traders' democracy, which, on June 13, had cried
out: "If they but dare to assail universal suffrage
. . . then . . . then we will show who we are!"
—they now consoled themselves with the thought
that the counter-revolutionary blow, which had
struck them, was no blow at all, and that the law
of May 31 was no law. On May 2, 1852, according to them, every Frenchman would appear
at the hustings, in one hand the ballot, in the

other the sword. With this prophecy they set
their hearts at ease. Finally, the Army was
punished by its superiors for the elections of
May and April, 1850, as it was punished for the
election of May 29, 1849. This time, however,
it said to itself determinately: "The revolution
shall not cheat us a third time."

The law of May 31, 1850, was the "coup d'état"
of the bourgeoisie. All its previous conquests
over the revolution had only a temporary character: 'they became uncertain the moment the
National Assembly stepped off the stage; they
depended upon the accident of general elections,
and the history of the elections since 1848 proved
irrefutably that, in the same measure as the
actual reign of the bourgeoisie gathered strength,
its moral reign over the masses wore off. Universal suffrage pronounced itself on May 10
pointedly against the reign of the bourgeoisie;
the bourgeoisie answered with the banishment
of universal suffrage. The law of May 31 was,
accordingly, one of the necessities of the class
struggle. On the other hand, the constitution
required a minimum of two million votes for the
valid election of the President of the republic.
If none of the Presidential candidates polled this
minimum, then the National Assembly was to
elect the President out of the three candidates
polling the highest votes. At the time that the
constitutive body made this law, ten million voters
were registered on the election rolls. In its
opinion, accordingly, one-fifth of the qualified
voters sufficed to make a choice for President
valid. The law of May 31 struck at least three
million voters off the rolls, reduced the number

of qualified voters to seven millions, and yet, notwithstanding, it kept the lawful minimum at two
millions for the election of a President. Accordingly, it raised the lawful minimum from a fifth
to almost a third of the qualified voters, i. e., it
did all it could to smuggle the Presidential election out of the hands of the people into those of
the National Assembly. Thus, by the election
law of May 31, the party of Order seemed to
have doubly secured its empire, in that it placed
the election of both the National Assembly and
the President of the republic in the keeping of
the stable portion of society.

V.

The strife immediately broke out again between the National Assembly and Bonaparte, so
soon as the revolutionary crisis was weathered,
and universal suffrage was abolished.

The Constitution had fixed the salary of Bonaparte at 600,000 francs. Barely half a year after
his installation, he succeeded in raising this sum
to its double: Odillon Barrot had wrung from
the constitutive assembly a yearly allowance of
600,000 francs for so-called representation ex-
penses. After June 13, Bonaparte hinted at
similar solicitations, to which, however, Barrot
then turned a deaf ear. Now, after May 31, he
forthwith utilized the favorable moment, and
caused his ministers to move a civil list of three
millions in the National Assembly. A long adventurous, vagabond career had gifted him with
the best developed antennae for feeling out the

weak moments when he could venture upon
squeezing money from his bourgeois. He carried on regular blackmail. The National Assembly had maimed the sovereignty of the people
with his aid and his knowledge: he now threatened to denounce its crime to the tribunal of
the people, if it did not pull out its purse and
buy his silence with three millions annually. It
had robbed three million Frenchmen of the suffrage: for every Frenchman thrown "out of circulation," he demanded a franc "in circulation."
He, the elect of six million, demanded indemnity
for the votes he had been subsequently cheated
of. The Committee of the National Assembly
turned the importunate fellow away. The Bonapartist press threatened: Could the National
Assembly break with the President of the republic at a time when it had broken definitely and on
principle with the mass of the nation? It rejected
the annual civil list, but granted, for this once,
an allowance of 2,160,000 francs. Thus it made
itself guilty of the double weakness of granting
the money, and, at the same time, showing by
its anger that it did so only unwillingly. We
shall presently see to what use Bonaparte put
the money. After this aggravating after-play,
that followed upon the heels of the abolition of
universal suffrage, and in which Bonaparte ex-
changed his humble attitude of the days of the
crisis of March and April for one of defiant
impudence towards the usurping parliament, the
National Assembly adjourned for three months,
from August 11, to November 11. It left behind in its place a Permanent Committee of 18
members that contained no Bonapartist, but did

contain a few moderate republicans. The Permanent Committee of the year 1849 had numbered only men of order and Bonapartists. At that time, however, the party of Order declared itself in permanence against the revolution; now the parliamentary republic declared itself in permanence against the President. After the law of May 31, only this rival still confronted the party of Order.

When the National Assembly reconvened in November, 1850, instead of its former petty skirmishes with the President, a great headlong struggle, a struggle for life between the two powers, seemed to have become inevitable.

As in the year 1849, the party of Order had, during this year's vacation, dissolved into its two separate factions, each occupied with its own restoration intrigues, which had received new impetus from the death of Louis Philippe. The Legitimist King, Henry V, had even appointed a regular Ministry, that resided in Paris, and in which sat members of the Permanent Committee. Hence, Bonaparte was, on his part, justified in making tours through the French Departments, and—according to the disposition of the towns that he happened to be gladdening with his presence—some times covertly, other times more openly blabbing out his own restoration plans, and gaining votes for himself. On these excursions, which the large official "Moniteur" and the small private "Moniteurs" of Bonaparte were, of course, bound to celebrate as triumphal marches, he was constantly accompanied by affiliated members of the "Society of December 10." This society dated from the year 1849. Under

the pretext of founding a benevolent association,
the slum-proletariat of Paris was organized into
secret sections, each section led by Bonapartist
agents, with a Bonapartist General at the head
of all. Along with ruined roués of questionable
means of support and questionable antecedents,
along with the foul and adventures-seeking dregs
of the bourgeoisie, there were vagabonds, dis-
mised soldiers, discharged convicts, runaway gal-
ley slaves, sharpers, jugglers, lazzaroni, pick-
pockets, sleight-of-hand performers, gamblers,
procurers, keepers of disorderly houses, porters,
literati, organ grinders, rag pickers, scissors
grinders, tinkers, beggars—in short, that whole
undefined, dissolute, kicked-about mass that the
Frenchmen style "la Bohéme." With this kindred element, Bonaparte formed the stock of the
"Society of December 10," a "benevolent association," in so far as, like Bonaparte himself, all
its members felt the need of being benevolent
to themselves at the expense of the toiling nation.
The Bonaparte, who here constitutes himself
Chief of the Slum-Proletariat; who only here
finds again in plenteous form the interests which
he personally pursues; who, in this refuse, offal
and wreck of all classes, recognizes the only class
upon which he can depend unconditionally:—this
is the real Bonaparte, the Bonaparte without
qualification. An old and crafty roué, he looks
upon the historic life of nations, upon their great
and public acts, as comedies in the ordinary sense,
as a carnival, where the great costumes, words
and postures serve only as masks for the pettiest
chicaneries. So, on the occasion of his expedition against Strassburg when a trained Swiss

vulture impersonated the Napoleonic eagle; so, again, on the occasion of his raid upon Boulogne, when he struck a few London lackeys into French uniform: they impersonated the army;[1] and so now, in his "Society of December 10," he collects 10,000 loafers who are to impersonate the people as Snug the Joiner does the lion. At a period when the bourgeoisie itself is playing the sheerest comedy, but in the most solemn manner in the world, without doing violence to any of the pedantic requirements of French dramatic etiquette, and is itself partly deceived by, partly convinced of, the solemnity of its own public acts, the adventurer, who took the comedy for simple comedy, was bound to win. Only after he has removed his solemn opponent, when he himself takes seriously his own role of emperor, and, with the Napoleonic mask on, imagines he impersonates the real Napoleon, only then does he become the victim of his own peculiar conception of history—the serious clown, who no longer takes history for a comedy, but a comedy for history. What the national work-shops were to the socialist workingmen, what the "Gardes mobiles" were to the bourgeois republicans, that was to Bonaparte the "Society of December 10," —a force for partisan warfare peculiar to himself. On his journeys, the divisions of the Society, packed away on the railroads, improvised an audience for him, performed public enthusiasm, shouted "vive l'Empereur," insulted and

---

[1] Under the reign of Louis Philippe, Bonaparte made two attempts to restore the throne of Napoleon: one in October, 1836, in an expedition from Switzerland upon Strassburg; and one in August, 1840, in an expedition from England upon Boulogne.

clubbed the republicans,—all, of course, under
the protection of the police. On his return stages
to Paris, this rable constituted his vanguard, it
forestalled or dispersed counter-demonstrations.
The "Society of December 10" belonged to him,
it was his own handiwork, his own thought.
Whatever else he appropriates, the power of circumstances places in his hands; whatever else
he does, either circumstances do for him, or he
is content to copy from the deeds of others; but
he, posing before the citizens with the official
phrases about "Order," "Religion," "Family,"
"Property," and, behind him, the secret society
of skipjacks and picaroons, the society of disorder, of prostitution, and of theft,—that is Bonaparte himself as the original author; and the
history of the "Society of December 10" is his
own history. Now, then, it happened that Representatives belonging to the party of order occa-
sionally got under the clubs of the Decembrists.
Nay, more. Police Commissioner Yon, who had
been assigned to the National Assembly, and was
charged with the guardianship of its safety, re-
ported to the Permanent Committee upon the testimony of one Alais, that a Section of the Decembrists had decided on the murder of General
Changarnier and of Dupin, the President of the
National Assembly, and had already settled upon
the men to execute the decree. One can imagine
the fright of Mr. Dupin. A parlimentary inquest
over the "Society of December 10," i. e., the pro-
fanation of the Bonapartist secret world, now
seemed inevitable. Just before the reconvening
of the National Assembly, Bonaparte circum-
spectly dissolved his Society, of course, on paper

only. As late as the end of 1851, Police Prefect Carlier vainly sought, in an exhaustive memorial, to move him to the real dissolution of the Decemberists.

The "Society of December 10" was to remain the private army of Bonaparte until he should have succeeded in converting the public Army into a "Society of December 10." Bonaparte made the first attempt in this direction shortly after the adjournment of the National Assembly, and he did so with the money which he had just wrung from it. As a fatalist, he lives devoted to the conviction that there are certain Higher Powers, whom man, particularly the soldier, cannot resist. First among these Powers he numbers cigars and champagne, cold poultry and garlic-sausage. Accordingly, in the apartments of the Elysée, he treated first the officers and under-officers to cigars and champagne, to cold poultry and garlic-sausage. On October 3, he repeats this manœuvre with the rank and file of the troops by the review of St. Maur; and, on October 10, the same manœuvre again, upon a larger scale, at the army parade of Satory. The Uncle bore in remembrance the campaigns of Alexander in Asia; the Nephew bore in remembrance the triumphal marches of Bacchus in the same country. Alexander was, indeed, a demigot; but Bacchus was a full-fledged god, and the patron deity, at that, of the "Society of December 10."

After the review of October 3, the Permanent Committee summoned the Minister of War, d'Hautpoul, before it. He promised that such breaches of discipline should not recur. We have

seen how, on October 10th, Bonaparte kept
d'Hautpoul's word. At both reviews Changarnier
had commanded as Commander-in-chief of the
Army of Paris. He, at once member of the Permanent Committee, Chief of the National Guard,
the "Savior" of January 29, and June 13, the
"Bulwark of Society," candidate of the Party
of Order for the office of President, the sus-
pected Monk of two monarchies,—he had never
acknowledged his subordination to the Minister
of War, had ever openly scoffed at the republican
Constitution, and had pursued Bonaparte with
a protection that was ambiguously distinguished.
Now he became zealous for the discipline in opposition to Bonaparte. While, on October 10, a
part of the cavalry cried: "Vive Napoléon!
Vivent les saucissons;"[2] Changarnier saw to it
that at least the infantry, which filed by under
the command of his friend Neumeyer, should
observe an icy silence. In punishment, the Minister of War, at the instigation of Bonaparte, deposed General Neumeyer from his post in Paris,
under the pretext of providing for him as Commander-in-chief of the Fourteenth and Fifteenth
Military Divisions. Neumeyer declined the exchange, and had, in consequence, to give his
resignation. On his part, Changarnier published
on November 2, an order, wherein he forbade the
troops to indulge, while under arms, in any sort
of political cries or demonstrations. The papers
devoted to the Elysée interests attacked Changarnier; the papers of the party of Order attacked
Bonaparte; the Permanent Committee held fre-
quent secret sessions, at which it was repeatedly

---

[2] Long live Napoleon! Long live the sausages!

proposed to declare the fatherland in danger; the Army seemed divided into two hostile camps, with two hostile staffs; one at the Elysée, where Bonaparte, the other at the Tuileries, where Changarnier resided. All that seemed wanting for the signal of battle to sound was the convening of the National Assembly. The French public looked upon the friction between Bonaparte and Changarnier in the light of the English journalist, who characterized it in these words: "The political servant girls of France are mopping away the glowing lava of the revolution with old mops, and they scold each other while doing their work."

Meanwhile Bonaparte hastened to depose the Minister of War, d'Hautpoul; to expedite him heels over head to Algiers; and to appoint in his place General Schramm as Minister of War. On November 12, he sent to the National Assembly a message of American excursiveness, overloaded with details, redolent of order, athirst for conciliation, resignful to the Constitution, dealing with all and everything, only not with the burning questions of the moment. As if in passing he dropped the words that according to the express provisions of the Constitution, the President alone disposes over the Army. The message closed with the following high-sounding protestations:

"France demands, above all things, peace . . . Alone bound by an oath, I shall keep myself within the narrow bounds marked out by it to me . . . As to me, elected by the people, and owing my power to it alone, I shall always submit to its lawfully expressed will. Should you at this session decide upon the revision of the Constitution, a Constitutional Convention will regulate the position of the Executive power. If you do not, then, the people will, in 1852, solemnly announce its decision. But, whatever the solution may be that the future has in store, let us arrive at an understanding to the end that never may passion, surprise or violence decide over the fate of a great nation. . . . That which, above all, bespeaks my attention is, not who will, in 1852, rule over France, but to so devote the time at my disposal that the interval may pass by without agitation and disturbance. I have straightforwardly opened my heart to you, you will answer my frankness with your confidence, my good efforts with your co-operation. God will do the rest."

The honnête, hypocritically temperate, commonplace-virtuous language of the bourgeoisie reveals its deep meaning in the mouth of the self-appointed ruler of the "Society of December 10," and of the picnic-hero of St. Maur and Satory.

The burgraves of the party of Order did not for a moment deceive themselves on the confidence that this unbosoming deserved. They were long blasé on oaths; they numbered among themselves veterans and virtuosi of perjury. The passage about the army did not, however, escape them. They observed with annoyance that the message, despite its prolix enumeration of the lately enacted laws, passed, with affected silence, over the most important of all, the election law, and, moreover, in case no revision of the Constitution was held, left the choice of the President, in 1852, with the people. The election law was the ball-and-chain to the feet of the party of Order, that hindered them from walking, and now assuredly from storming. Furthermore, by the official disbandment of the "Society of December 10," and the dismissal of the Minister of War, d'Hautpoul, Bonaparte had, with his own hands, sacrificed the scape-goats on the altar of the fatherland. He had turned off the expected collision. Finally, the party of Order itself anxiously sought to avoid every decisive conflict with the Executive, to weaken and to blur it over. Fearing to lose its conquests over the revolution, it let its rival gather the fruits thereof. "France demands, above all things, peace,"— with this language had the party of Order been apostrophizing the revolution, since February; with this language did Bonaparte's message now apostrophize the party of Order: "France demands, above all things, peace." Bonaparte committed acts that aimed at usurpation, but the party of Order committed a "disturbance of the peace," if it raised the hue and cry, and explained them hypochondriacally. The sausages of Satory were mouse-still when nobody talked about them;—"France demands, above all things, peace." Accordingly, Bonaparte demanded that he be let alone; and the parliamentary party was lamed with a double fear: the fear of re-conjuring up the revolutionary disturbance of the peace, and the fear of itself appearing as the disturber of the peace in the eyes of its own class, of the bourgeoisie. Seeing that, above all things, France demanded peace, the party of Order did not dare, after Bonaparte

had said "peace" in his message, to answer "war."
The public, who had promised to itself the pleasure of seeing great scenes of scandal at the opening of the National Assembly, was cheated out of its expectations. The opposition deputies, who demanded the submission of the minutes of the Permanent Committee over the October occurrences, were outvoted. All debate that might excite was fled from on principle. The labors of the National Assembly during November and December, 1850, were without interest.

Finally, toward the end of December, began a guerilla warfare about certain prerogatives of the parliament. The movement sank into the mire of petty chicaneries on the prerogative of the two powers, since, with the abolition of universal suffrage, the bourgeoisie had done away with the class struggle.

A judgment for debt had been secured against Mauguin, one of the Representatives. Upon inquiry by the President of the Court, the Minister of Justice, Rouher, declared that an order of arrest should be made out without delay. Mauguin was, accordingly, cast into the debtors' prison. The National Assembly bristled up when it heard of the "attentat." It not only ordered his immediate release, but had him forcibly taken out of Clichy the same evening by its own greffier. In order, nevertheless, to shield its belief in the "sacredness of private property." and also with the ulterior thought of opening, in case of need, an asylum for troublesome Mountainers, it declared the imprisonment of a Representative for debt to be permissible upon its previous consent. It forgot to decree that the

President also could be locked up for debt. By
its act, it wiped out the last semblance of inviolability that surrounded the members of its
own body.

It will be remembered that, upon the testimony
of one Allais, Police Commissioner Yon had
charged a Section of Decembrists with a plan to
murder Dupin and Changarnier. With an eye
upon that, the questors proposed at the very first
session, that the parliament organize a police
force of its own, paid for out of the private
budget of the National Assembly itself, and
wholly independent of the Police Prefects. The
Minister of the Interior, Baroche, protested
against this trespass on his preserves. A miserable compromise followed, according to which
the Police Commissioner of the Assembly was
to be paid out of its own private budget and
was to be subject to the appointment and dismissal of its own questors, but only upon previous agreement with the Minister of the Interior. In the meantime Allais had been prose-
cuted by the Government. It was an easy thing,
in Court, to present his testimony in the light of
a mystification, and, through the mouth of the
Public Prosecutor, to throw Dupin, Changarnier,
Yon, together with the whole National Assembly,
into a ridiculous light. Thereupon, on December 29, Minister Baroche writes a letter to Dupin,
in which he demands the dismissal of Yon. The
Committee of the National Assembly decides
to keep Yon in office; nevertheless, the National
Assembly, frightened by its own violence in the
affair of Mauguin, and accustomed, every time
it has shied a blow at the Executive, to receive

back from it two in exchange, does not sanction this decision. It dismisses Yon in reward for his zeal in office, and robs itself of a parliamentary prerogative, indispensable against a person who does not decide by night to execute by day, but decides by day and executes by night.

We have seen how, during the months of November and December, under great and severe provocations, the National Assembly evaded and refused the combat with the Executive power. Now we see it compelled to accept it on the smallest occasions. In the affair of Mauguin, it confirms in principle the liability of a Representative to imprisonment for debt, but to itself reserves the power of allowing the principle to be applied only to the Representatives whom it dislikes,— and for this infamous privilege we see it wrangling with the Minister of Justice. Instead of utilizing the alleged murder plan to the end of fastening an inquest upon the "Society of December 10," and of exposing Bonaparte beyond redemption before France and Europe in his true figure, as the head of the slum-proletariat of Paris, it allows the collision to sink to a point where the only issue between itself and the Minister of the Interior is, Who has jurisdiction over the appointment and dismissal of a Police Commissioner? Thus we see the party of Order, during this whole period, compelled by its ambiguous position to wear out and fritter away its conflict with the Executive power in small quarrels about jurisdiction, in chicaneries, in pettifogging, in boundary disputes, and to turn the stalest questions of form into the very substance of its activity. It dares not accept the collision

at the moment when it involves a principle, when
the Executive power has really given itself a
blank, and when the cause of the National Assembly would be the cause of the nation. It
would thereby have issued to the nation an order
of march; and it feared nothing so much as that
the nation should move. Hence, on these occasions, it rejects the motions of the Mountain,
and proceeds to the order of the day. After the
issue has in this way lost all magnitude, the Executive power quietly awaits the moment when
it can take it up again upon small and insignificant occasions; when, so to say, the issue offers
only a parliamentary local interest. Then does
the repressed valor of the party of Order break
forth, then it tears away the curtain from the
scene, then it denounces the President, then it
declares the republic to be in danger,—but then
all its pathos appears stale, and the occasion for
the quarrel a hypocritical pretext, or not at all
worth the effort. The parliamentary tempest becomes a tempest in a tea-pot, the struggle an
intrigue, the collision a scandal. While the revolutionary classes gloat with sardonic laughter
over the humiliation of the National Assembly—
they, of course, being as enthusiastic for the prerogatives of the parliament as that body is for
public freedom—the bourgeoisie, outside of the
parliament, does not understand how the bourgeoisie, inside of the parliament, can squander
its time with such petty bickerings, and can en-
danger peace by such wretched rivalries with the
President. It is puzzled at a strategy that makes
peace the very moment everybody expects bat-

tles, and that attacks the very moment everybody believes peace has been concluded.

On December 20, Pascal Duprat interpellated the Minister of the Interior on the "Goldbar Lottery." This lottery was a "Daughter from Elysium"; Bonaparte, together with his faithful, had given her birth; and Police Prefect Carlier had placed her under his official protection, although the French law forbade all lotteries, with the exception of raffles for benevolent purposes. Seven million tickets, a franc a piece, and the profit ostensibly destined to the shipping of Parisian vagabonds to California. Golden dreams were to displace the Socialist dreams of the Parisian proletariat; the tempting prospect of a prize was to displace the doctrinal right to labor. Of course, the workingmen of Paris did not recognize in the lustre of the California gold bars the lack-lustre francs that had been wheedled out of their pockets. In the main, however, the scheme was an unmitigated swindle. The vagabonds, who meant to open California gold mines without taking the pains to leave Paris, were Bonaparte himself and his Round Table of desperate insolvents. The three millions granted by the National Assembly were rioted away; the Treasury had to be refilled somehow or another. In vain did Bonaparte open a national subscription, at the head of which he himself figured with a large sum, for the establishment of so-called "cités ouvrières."[3] The hard-hearted bourgeois waited, distrustful, for the payment of his own shares; and, as this, of course, never took place, the speculation in Socialist castles in the

---

[3] Work cities.

air fell flat. The gold bars drew better. Bonaparte and his associates did not content themselves with putting into their own pockets part of the surplus of the seven millions over and above the bars that were to be drawn; they manufactured false tickets; they sold, of Number 10 alone, fifteen to twenty lots—a financial operation fully in the spirit of the "Society of December 10"! The National Assembly did not here have before it the fictitious President of the Republic, but Bonaparte himself in flesh and blood. Here it could catch him in the act, not in conflict with the Constitution, but with the penal code. When, upon Duprat's interpellation, the National Assembly went over to the order of the day, this did not happen simply because Girardin's motion to declare itself "satisfied" reminded the party of Order of its own systematic corruption: the bourgeois, above all the bourgeois who has been inflated into a statesman, supplements his practical meanness with theoretical pompousness. As statesman, he becomes, like the Government facing him, a superior being, who can be fought only in a higher, more exalted manner.

Bonaparte—who, for the very reason of his being a "bohemian," a princely slum-proletarian, had over the scampish bourgeois the advantage that he could carry on the fight after the Assembly itself had carried him with its own hands over the slippery ground of the military banquets, of the reviews, of the "Society of December 10," and, finally, of the penal code—now saw that the moment had arrived when he could move from the seemingly defensive to the offensive. He was but little troubled by the intermediate and

trifling defeats of the Minister of Justice, of the
Minister of War, of the Minister of the Navy,
of the Minister of Finance, whereby the National
Assembly indicated its growling displeasure. Not
only did he prevent the Ministers from resigning,
and thus recognizing the subordination of the
executive power to the Parliament; he could now
accomplish what during the vacation of the National Assembly he had commenced, the separa-
tion of the military power from the Assembly—
the deposition of Changarnier.

An Elysée paper published an order, issued
during the month of May, ostensibly to the First
Military Division, and, hence, proceeding from
Changarnier, wherein the officers were recom-
mended, in case of an uprising, to give no quarter to the traitors in their own ranks, to shoot
them down on the spot, and to refuse troops to
the National Assembly, should it make a requisition for such. On January 3, 1851, the Cabinet
was interpellated on this order. The Cabinet
demands for the examination of the affair at
first three months, then one week, finally only
twenty-four hours' time. The Assembly orders
an immediate explanation. Changarnier rises and
declares that this order never existed; he adds
that he would ever hasten to respond to the calls
of the National Assembly, and that, in case of a
collision, they could count upon him. The Assembly receives his utterances with inexpressible
applause, and decrees a vote of confidence to him.
It thereby resign its own powers; it decrees its
own impotence and the omnipotence of the Army
by committing itself to the private protection of
a general. But the general, in turn, deceives

himself when he places at the Assembly's dis
posal and against Bonaparte a power that he
holds only as a fief from that same Bonaparte
and when, on his part, he expects protection from
this Parliament, from his protégé, itself needfu
of protection. But Changarnier has faith in the
mysterious power with which since January
1849, he had been clad by the bourgeoisie. He
takes himself for the Third Power, standing be
side the other Powers of Government. He share:
the faith of all the other heroes, or rather saints
of this epoch, whose greatness consists but ir
the interested good opinion that their own party
holds of them, and who shrink into every-day
figures so soon as circumstances invite them to
perform miracles. Infidelity is, indeed, the deadly
enemy of these supposed heroes and real saints
Hence their virtuously proud indignation at the
unenthusiastic wits and scoffers.

That same evening the Ministers were summoned to the Elysée; Bonaparte presses the removal of Changarnier; five Ministers refuse to
sign the order; the "Moniteur" announces a Ministerial crisis; and the party of Order threatens
the formation of a Parliamentary army under
the command of Changarnier. The party of
Order had the constitutional power hereto. It
needed only to elect Changarnier President of the
National Assembly in order to make a requisition
for whatever military forces it needed for its own
safety. It could do this all the more safely, seeing that Changarnier still stood at the head of
the Army and of the Parisian National Guard
and only lay in wait to be summoned, together
with the Army. The Bonapartist press did not

even dare to question the right of the National
Assembly to issue a direct requisition for troops;
—a legal scruple, that, under the given circumstances, did not promise success. That the Army
would have obeyed the orders of the National
Assembly is probable, when it is considered that
Bonaparte had to look eight days all over Paris
to find two generals—Baraguay d'Hilliers and
St. Jean d'Angley—who declared themselves
ready to countersign the order cashiering Changarnier. That, however, the party of Order
would have found in its own ranks and in the
parliament the requisite vote for such a decision
is more than doubtful, when it is considered
that, eight days later, 286 votes pulled away from
it, and that, as late as December, 1851, at the
last decisive hour, the Mountain rejected a similar proposition. Nevertheless, the burgraves
might still have succeeded in driving the mass of
their party to an act of heroism, consisting in
feeling safe behind a forest of bayonets, and in
accepting the services of the Army, which found
itself deserted in its camp. Instead of this, the
Messieurs Burgraves betook themselves to the
Elysée on the evening of January 6, with the
view of inducing Bonaparte, by means of politic
words and considerations, to drop the removal of
Changarnier. Him whom we must convince we
recognize as the master of the situation. Bonaparte, made to feel secure by this step, appoints
on January 12 a new Ministry, in which the leaders of the old, Fould and Baroche, are retained.
St. Jean d'Angley becomes Minister of War;
the "Moniteur" announces the decree cashiering
Changarnier; his command is divided up between

Baraguay d'Hilliers, who receives the First Division, and Perrot, who is placed over the National Guard. The "Bulwark of Society" is turned down; and, although no dog barks over the event, in the Bourses the stock quotations rise.

By repelling the Army, that, in Changarnier's person, put itself at its disposal, and thus irrevocably stood up against the President, the party of Order declares that the bourgeoisie has lost its vocation to reign. Already there was no parliamentary Ministry. By losing, furthermore the handle to the Army and to the National Guard, what instrument of force was there left to the National Assembly in order to maintain both the usurped power of the parliament over the people, and its constitutional power over the President? None. All that was left to it was the appeal to peaceful principles, that itself had always explained as "general rules" merely, to be prescribed to third parties, and only in order to enable itself to move all the more freely. With the removal of Changarnier, with the transfer of the military power to Bonaparte, closes the first part of the period that we are considering the period of the struggle between the party of Order and the Executive power. The war between the two powers is now openly declared; it is conducted openly; but only after the party of Order has lost both arms and soldiers. Without a Ministry, without any army, without a people, without the support of public opinion; since its election law of May 31, no longer the representative of the sovereign nation; sans eyes, sans ears, sans teeth, sans everything, the National

Assembly had gradually converted itself into a French Parliament of olden days, that must leave all action to the Government, and content itself with growling remonstrances "post festum." [*]

The party of Order receives the new Ministry with a storm of indignation. General Bedeau calls to mind the mildness of the Permanent Committee during the vacation, and the excessive prudence with which it had renounced the privilege of disclosing its minutes. Now, the Minister of the Interior himself insists upon the disclosure of these minutes, that have now, of course, become dull as stagnant waters, reveal no new facts, and fall without making the slightest effect upon the blasé public. Upon Remusat's proposition, the National Assembly retreats into its Committees, and appoints a "Committee on Extraordinary Measures." Paris steps all the less out of the ruts of its daily routine, seeing that business is prosperous at the time, the manufactories busy, the prices of cereals low, provisions abundant, the savings banks receiving daily new deposits. The "extraordinary measures," that the parliament so noisily announced, fizzle out on January 18 in a vote of lack of confidence against the Ministry, without General Changarnier's name being even mentioned. The party of Order was forced to frame its motion in that way so as to secure the votes of the republicans, because, of all the acts of the Ministry, Changarnier's dismissal only was the very one they approved, while the party of Order cannot, in fact, condemn the other Ministerial acts which it had itself dictated.

The January 18 vote of lack of confidence

---

[*] After the act is done; after the feast.

was decided by 415 ayes against 286 nays. It
was, accordingly, put through by a coalition of
the uncompromising Legitimists and Orleanists
with the pure republicans and the Mountain.
Thus it revealed the fact that, in its conflicts with
Bonaparte, the party of Order had lost, not only
the Ministry, not only the Army, but also its independent parliamentary majority; that a troop
of Representatives had deserted its camp out of
a fanatic zeal for harmony, out of fear of fight,
out of lassitude, out of family considerations for
the salaries of relatives in office, out of specula-
tions on vacancies in the Ministry (Odillon Barrot), or out of that unmitigated selfishness that
causes the average bourgeois to be ever inclined
to sacrifice the interests of his class to this or
that private motive. The Bonapartist Representatives belonged from the start to the party of
Order only in the struggle against the revolution.
The leader of the Catholic party, Montalembert,
already then threw his influence in the scale of
Bonaparte, since he despaired of the vitality of
the parliamentary party. Finally, the leaders of
this party itself, Thiers and Berryer—the Orleanist and the Legitimist—were compelled to
proclaim themselves openly as republicans; to
admit that their heart favored royalty, but their
head the republic: that their parliamentary republic was the only possible form for the rule
of the bourgeoisie. Thus were they compelled
to brand, before the eyes of the bourgeois class
itself, as an intrigue—as dangerous as it was
senseless—the restoration plans, which they continued to pursue indefatigably behind the back
of the parliament.

The January 18 vote of lack of confidence struck the Ministers, not the President. But it was not the Ministry, it was the President who had deposed Changarnier. Should the party of Order place Bonaparte himself under charges? On account of his restoration hankerings? These only supplemented their own. On account of his conspiracy at the military reviews and of the "Society of December 10"? They had long since buried these subjects under simple orders of business. On account of the discharge of the hero of January 29 and June 13, of the man who, in May, 1850, threatened, in case of riot, to set Paris on fire at all its four corners? Their allies of the Mountain and Cavaignac did not even allow them to console the fallen "Bulwark of Society" with an official testimony of their sympathy. They themselves could not deny the constitutional right of the President to remove a General. They stormed only because he made an unparliamentary use of his constitutional right. Had they not themselves constantly made an unconstitutional use of their parliamentary prerogative, notably by the abolition of universal suffrage? Consequently they were reminded to move exclusively within parliamentary bounds. Indeed, it required that peculiar disease, a disease that, since 1848, has raged over the whole continent, "Parliamentary Idiocy,"—that fetters those whom it infects to an imaginary world, and robs them of all sense, all remembrance, all understanding of the rude outside world;—it required this "Parliamentary Idiocy" in order that the party of Order, which had, with its own hands, destroyed all the conditions for parliamentary power, and, in its struggle with the other classes, was obliged to destroy them, still should consider its parliamentary victories as victories, and imagine it hit the President by striking his Ministers. They only afforded him an opportunity to humble the National Assembly anew in the eyes of the nation. On January 20, the "Moniteur" announced that the dismissal of the whole Ministry was accepted. Under the pretext that none of the parliamentary parties had any longer the majority—as proved by the January 18 vote, that fruit of the coalition between Mountain and royalists—, and, in order to await the re-formation of a majority, Bonaparte appointed a so-called transition Ministry, of whom no member belonged to the parliament—altogether wholly unknown and insignificant individuals; a Ministry of mere clerks and secretaries. The party of Order could now wear itself out in the game with these puppets; the Executive power no longer considered it worth the while to be seriously represented in the National Assembly. By this act Bonaparte concentrated the whole executive power all the more securely in his own person; he had all the freer elbow-room to exploit the same to his own ends, the more his Ministers became mere supernumaries.

The party of Order, now allied with the Mountain, revenged itself by rejecting the Presidential endowment project of 1,800,000 francs, which the chief of the "Society of December 10" had compelled his Ministerial clerks to present to the 'Assembly. This time a majority of only 102 votes carried the day; accordingly, since January 18, 27 more votes had fallen off; the dissolution of the party of Order was making progress. Lest any one might for a moment be deceived touching the meaning of its coalition with the Mountain, the party of Order simultaneously scorned even to consider a motion, signed by 189 members of the Mountain, for a general amnesty to political criminals. It was enough that the Minister of the Interior, one Baissé, declared that the national tranquility was only in appearance, in secret there reigned deep agitation, in secret, ubiquitous societies were organized, the democratic papers were preparing to re-appear, the reports from the Departments were unfavorable, the fugitives of Geneva conducted a conspiracy via Lyons through the whole of southern France, France stood on the verge of an industrial and commercial crisis, the manufacturers of Roubaix were working shorter hours, the prisoners of Belle Isle had mutinied;—it was enough that even a mere Baissé should conjure up the "Red Spectre" for the party of Order to reject without discussion a motion that would have gained for the National Assembly a tremendous popularity, and thrown Bonaparte back into its arms. Instead of allowing itself to be intimidated by the Executive power with the perspective of fresh disturbances, the party of Order should rather have allowed a little elbow-room to the class struggle, in order to secure the dependence of the Executive upon itself. But it did not feel itself equal to the task of playing with fire.

Meanwhile, the so-called transition Ministry vegetated along until the middle of April. Bonaparte tired out and fooled the National Assembly with constantly new Ministerial combina-

tions. Now he seemed to intend constructing
a republican Ministry with Lamartine and Bil-
lault; then, a parliamentary one with the inevitable Odillon Barrot, whose name must never be
absent when a dupe is needed; then again, a
Legitimist, with Batismenil and Benoist d'Azy;
and yet again, an Orleansist, with Malleville.
While thus throwing the several factions of the
party of Order into strained relations with one
another, and alarming them all with the prospect
of a republican Ministry, together with the thereupon inevitable restoration of universal suffrage,
Bonaparte simultaneously raises in the bourgeoisie the conviction that his sincere efforts for
a parliamentary Ministry are wrecked upon the
irreconcilable antagonism of the royalist factions. All the while the bourgeoisie was clamor-
ing louder and louder for a "'strong Government," and was finding it less and less pardon-
able to leave France "without an administration," in proportion as a general commercial
crisis seemed to be under way and making re-
cruits for Socialism in the cities, as did the ruin-
ously low price of grain in the rural districts.
Trade became daily duller; the unemployed hands
increased perceptibly; in Paris, at least 10,000
workingmen were without bread; in Rouen,
Muehlhausen, Lyons, Roubaix, Tourcoign, St.
Etienne, Elbeuf, etc., numerous factories stood
idle. Under these circumstances Bonaparte could
venture to restore, on April 11, the Ministry of
January 18; Messieurs Rouher, Fould, Baroche,
etc., reinforced by Mr. Léon Faucher, whom the
constitutive assembly had, during its last days,
unanimously, with the exception of five Ministe-

rial votes, branded with a vote of censure for circulating false telegraphic dispatches. Accordingly, the National Assembly had won a victory on January 18 over the Ministry, it had, for the period of three months, been battling with Bonaparte, and all this merely to the end that, on April 11, Fould and Baroche should be able to take up the Puritan Faucher as third in their ministerial league.

In November, 1849, Bonaparte had satisfied himself with an *Unparliamentary*, in January, 1851, with an *Extra-Parliamentary*, on April 11, he felt strong enough to form an *Anti-Parliamentary* Ministry, that harmoniously combined within itself the votes of lack of confidence of both assemblies—the constitutive and the legislative, the republican and the royalist. This ministerial progression was a thermometer by which the parliament could measure the ebbing temperature of its own life. This had sunk so low by the end of April that, at a personal interview, Persigny could invite Changarnier to go over to the camp of the President. Bonaparte, he assured Changarnier, considered the influence of the National Assembly to be wholly annihilated, and already the proclamation was ready, that was to be published after the steadily contemplated, but again accidentally postponed "coup d'état." Changarnier communicated this announcement of its death to the leaders of the party of Order; but who was there to believe a bed-bug bite could kill? The parliament, however beaten, however dissolved, however death-tainted it was, could not persuade itself to see, in the duel with the grotesque chief of the "Society

of December 10," anything but a duel with a
bed-bug. But Bonaparte answered the party of
Order as Agesilaus did King Agis: "I seem to
you an ant; but shall one day be a lion."

VI

The coalition with the Mountain and the pure
republicans, to which the party of Order found
itself condemned in its fruitless efforts to keep
possession of the military and to reconquer supreme control over the Executive power, proved
conclusively that it had forfeited its independent
parliamentary majority. The calendar and clock
merely gave, on May 29, the signal for its complete dissolution. With May 29 commenced the
last year of the life of the National Assembly. It
now had to decide for the unchanged continuance
or the revision of the Constitution. But a revision of the Constitution meant not only the de-
finitive supremacy of either the bourgeoisie or
the small traders' democracy, of either democracy
or proletarian anarchy, of either a parliamentary
republic or Bonaparte, it meant also either Orleans or Bourbon! Thus fell into the very
midst of the parliament the apple of discord,
around which the conflict of interests, that cut
up the party of Order into hostile factions, was
to kindle into an open conflagration. The party
of Order was a combination of heterogeneous social substances. The question of revision raised
a political temperature, in which the product was
reduced to its original components.

The interest of the Bonapartists in the revision

was simple: they were above all concerned in the abolition of Article 45, which forbade Bonaparte's re-election and the prolongation of his term. Not less simple seemed to be the position of the republicans; they rejected all revision, seeing in that only a general conspiracy against the republic; as they disposed over more than one-fourth of the votes in the National Assembly, and, according to the Constitution, a three-fourths majority was requisite to revise and to call a revisory convention, they needed only to count their own votes to be certain of victory. Indeed, they were certain of it.

Over and against these clear-cut positions, the party of Order found itself tangled in inextricable contradictions. If it voted against the revision, it endangered the "status quo," by leaving to Bonaparte only one expedient—that of violence and handing France over, on May 2, 1852, at the very time of election, a prey to revolutionary anarchy, with a President whose authority was at an end, with a parliament that the party had long ceased to own, and with a people that it meant to re-conquer. If it voted constitutionally for a revision, it knew that it voted in vain, and would constitutionally have to go under before the veto of the republicans. If, unconstitutionally, it pronounced a simple majority binding, it could hope to control the revolution only in case it surrendered unconditionally to the domination of the Executive power: it then made Bonaparte master of the Constitution, of the revision and of itself. A merely partial revision, prolonging the term of the President, opened the way to imperial usurpation;

a general revision, shortening the existence of
the republic, threw the dynastic claims into an
inevitable conflict: the conditions for a Bourbon
and those for an Orleanist restoration were not
only different, they mutually excluded each other.

The parliamentary republic was more than
a neutral ground on which the two factions
of the French bourgeoisie—Legitimists and Orleanists, large landed property and manufacture
—could lodge together with equal rights. It
was the indispensable condition for their common
reign, the only form of government in which
their common class interest could dominate both
the claims of their separate factions and all the
other classes of society. As royalists, they re-
lapsed into their old antagonism: into the struggle for the overlordship of either landed property or of money; and the highest expression
of this antagonism, its personification, were the
two kings themselves, their dynasties. Hence the
resistance of the party of Order to the recall of
the Bourbons.

The Orleanist Representative Creton moved
periodically in 1849, 1850 and 1851 the repeal
of the decree of banishment against the royal
families; as periodically did the parliament present the spectacle of an Assembly of royalists
who stubbornly shut to their banished kings the
door through which they could return home.
Richard III. murdered Henry VI, with the remark that he was too good for this world, and
belonged in heaven. They declared France too
bad to have her kings back again. Forced by
the power of circumstances, they had become re-

publicans, and repeatedly sanctioned the popular
mandate that exiled their kings from France.

The revision of the Constitution, and circumstances compelled its consideration, at once made
uncertain not only the republic itself, but also the
joint reign of the two bourgeois factions; and
it revived, with the possibility of the monarchy,
both the rivalry of interests which these two factions had alternately allowed to preponderate,
and the struggle for the supremacy of the one
over the other. The diplomats of the party of
Order believed they could allay the struggle by
a combination of the two dynasties through a so-
called fusion of the royalist parties and their
respective royal houses. The true fusion of the
restoration and the July monarchy was, however,
the parliamentary republic, in which the Orleanist and Legitimist colors were dissolved, and the
bourgeois species vanished in the plain bourgeois, in the bourgeois genus. Now, however,
the plan was to turn the Orleanist Legitimist
and the Legitimist Orleanist. The kingship, in
which their antagonism was personified, was to
incarnate their unity; the expression of their exclusive faction interests was to become the expression of their common class interest; the monarchy was to accomplish what only the abolition
of two monarchies—the republic—could and did
accomplish. This was the philosopher's stone,
for the finding of which the doctors of the party
of Order were breaking their heads. As though
the Legitimate monarchy ever could be the monarchy of the industrial bourgeoisie, or the bourgeois monarchy the monarchy of the hereditary
landed aristocracy! As though landed property

and industry could fraternize under one crown,
where the crown could fall only upon one head,
the head of the older or the younger brother! As
though industry could at all deal upon a footing
of equality with landed property, so long as landed property did not decide itself to become industrial. If Henry V. were to die tomorrow,
the Count of Paris would not, therefore, become
the king of the Legitimists, unless he ceased to
be the King of the Orleanists. Nevertheless,
the fusion philosophers, who became louder in
the measure that the question of revision stepped
to the fore, who had provided themselves with a
daily organ in the "Assemblée Nationale," who,
even at this very moment (February, 1852) are
again at work, explained the whole difficulty by
the opposition and rivalries of the two dynasties.
The attempts to reconcile the family of Orleans
with Henry V., begun since the death of Louis
Philippe, but, as all these dynastic intrigues carried on only during the vacation of the National
Assembly, between acts, behind the scenes, more
as a sentimental coquetry with the old superstition than as a serious affair, were now raised by
the party of Order to the dignity of a great
State question, and were conducted upon the
public stage, instead of, as heretofore, in the
amateurs' theater. Couriers flew from Paris to
Venice, from Venice to Claremont, from Claremont to Paris. The Duke of Chambord issues
a manifesto in which he announces, not his own,
but the "national" restoration, "with the aid of
all the members of his family." The Orleanist
Salvandy throws himself at the feet of Henry
V. The Legitimist leaders Berryer, Benoit d'Azy,

St. Priest travel to Claremont, to persuade the Orleans, but in vain. The fusionists learn too late that the interests of the two bourgeois factions neither lose in exclusiveness nor gain in pliancy where they sharpen to a point in the form of family interests, of the interests of the two royal houses. When Henry V. recognized the Count of Paris as his successor—the only success that the fusion could at best score—the house of Orleans acquired no claim that the childlessness of Henry V. had not already secured to it; but, on the other hand, it lost all the claims that it had conquered by the July revolution. It renounced its original claims, all the title, that, during a struggle nearly one hundred years long, it had wrested from the older branch of the Bourbons; it bartered away its historic prerogative, the prerogative of its family-tree. Fusion, accordingly, amounted to nothing else than the resignation of the house of Orleans, its Legitimist resignation, a repentful return from the Protestant State Church into the Catholic;—a return, at that, that did not even place it on the throne that it had lost, but on the steps of the throne on which it was born. The old Orleanist Ministers Guizot, Duchatel, etc., who likewise hastened to Claremont, to advocate the fusion, represented in fact only the nervous reaction of the July monarchy; despair, both in the citizen kingdom and the kingdom of citizens; the superstitious belief in legitimacy as the last amulet against anarchy. Mediators, in their imagination, between Orleans and Bourbon, they were in reality but apostate Orleanists, and as such were they received by the Prince of Joinville. The virile,

bellicose part of the Orleanists, on the contrary—
Thiers, Baze, etc.—, persuaded the family of
Louis Philippe all the easier that, seeing every
plan for the immediate restoration of the monarchy presupposed the fusion of the two dynasties, and every plan for fusion the resignation
of the house of Orleans, it corresponded, on the
contrary, wholly with the tradition of its ancestors to recognize the republic for the time
being, and to wait until circumstances permitted
the conversion of the Presidential chair into a
throne. Joinville's candidacy was set afloat as a
rumor, public curiosity was held in suspense,
and a few months later, after the revision was rejected, openly proclaimed in September.

Accordingly, the essay of a royalist fusion between Orleanists and Legitimists did not mis-
carry only, it broke up their parliamentary fusion, the republican form that they had adopted
in common, and it decomposed the party of Order
into its original components. But the wider
the breach became between Venice and Claremont, the further they drifted away from each
other, and the greater the progress made by the
Joinville agitation, all the more active and earnest became the negotiations between Faucher,
the Minister of Bonaparte, and the Legitimists.

The dissolution of the party of Order went
beyond its original elements. Each of the two
large factions fell in turn into new fragments.
It was as if all the old political shades, that formerly fought and crowded one another within
each of the two circles—be it that of the Legitimists or that of the Orleanists—, had been
thawed out like dried infusoria by contact with

water; as if they had recovered enough vitality to build their own groups and assert their own antagonisms. The Legitimists dreamed they were back amidst the quarrels between the Tuileries and the pavilion Marsan, between Villèle and Polignac; the Orleanists lived anew through the golden period of the tourneys between Guizot, Molé, Broglie, Thiers, and Odillon Barrot.

That portion of the party of Order—eager for a revision of the Constitution but disagreed upon the extent of revision—made up of the Legitimists under Berryer and Falloux and of those under Laroche Jacquelein, together with the tired-out Orleanists under Molé, Broglie, Montalembert and Odillon Barrot, united with the Bonapartist Representatives in the following indefinite and loosely drawn motion:

"The undersigned Representatives, with the end in view of restoring to the nation the full exercise of her sovereignty, move that the Constitution be revised."

At the same time, however, they unanimously declared through their spokesman, Tocqueville, that the National Assembly had not the right to move the abolition of the republic, that right being vested only in a Constitutional Convention. For the rest, the Constitution could be revised only in a "legal" way, that is to say, only in case a three-fourths majority decided in favor of revision, as prescribed by the Constitution. After a six days' stormy debate, the revision was rejected on July 19, as was to be foreseen. In its favor 446 votes were cast, against it 278. The resolute Orleanists, Thiers, Changarnier, etc., voted with the republicans and the Mountain.

Thus the majority of the parliament pronounced itself against the Constitution, while the Constituion itself pronounced itself for the minority, and its decision binding. But had not the party of Order on May 31, 1850, had it not on June 13, 1849, subordinated the Constitution to the parliamentary majority? Did not the whole republic they had been hitherto having rest upon the subordination of the Constitutional clauses to the majority decisions of the parliament? Had they not left to the democrats the Old Testament superstitious belief in the letter of the law, and had they not chastised the democrats therefor? At this moment, however, revision meant nothing else than the continuance of the Presidential power, as the continuance of the Constitution meant nothing else than the deposition of Bonaparte. The parliament had pronounced itself for him, but the Constitution pronounced itself against the parliament. Accordingly, he acted both in the sense of the parliament when he tore up the Constitution, and in the sense of the Constitution when he chased away the parliament.

The parliament pronounced the Constitution, and, thereby, also, its own reign, "outside of the pale of the majority"; by its decision, it repealed the Constitution, and continued the Presidential power, and it at once declared that neither could the one live nor the other die so long as itself existed. The feet of those who were to bury it stood at the door. While it was debating the subject of revision, Bonaparte removed General Baraguay d'Hilliers, who showed himself irresolute, from the command of the First Military Division, and appointed in his place General Mag-

nan, the conqueror of Lyon, the hero of the
December days, one of his own creatures, who,
already under Louis Philippe, on the occasion of
the Boulogne expedition, had somewhat compromised himself in his favor.

By its decision on the revision, the party of
Order proved that it knew neither how to rule
nor how to obey; neither how to live nor how to
die; neither how to bear with the republic nor
how to overthrow it; neither how to maintain the
Constitution nor how to throw it overboard:
neither how to co-operate with the President nor
how to break with him. From what quarter
did it then, look to for the solution of all the
existing perplexities? From the calendar, from
the course of events. It ceased to assume the
control of events. It, accordingly, invited events
to don its authority and also the power to which
in its struggle with the people, it had yielded
one attribute after another until it finally stood
powerless before the same. To the end that the
Executive be able all the more freely to formu-
late his plan of campaign against it, strengthen
his means of attack, choose his tools, fortify his
positions, the party of Order decided, in the very
midst of this critical moment, to step off the stage,
and adjourn for three months, from August 10
to November 4.

Not only was the parliamentary party dissolved into its two great factions, not only was
each of these dissolved within itself, but the
party of Order, inside of the parliament, was
at odds with the party of Order, outside of the
parliament. The learned speakers and writers
of the bourgeoisie, their tribunes and their press,

in short, the ideologists of the bourgeoisie and the bourgeoisie itself, the representatives and the represented, stood estranged from, and no longer understood one another.

The Legitimists in the provinces, with their cramped horizon and their boundless enthusiasm, charged their parliamentary leaders Berryer and Falloux with desertion to the Bonapartist camp, and with apostacy from Henry V. Their lily-mind[1] believed in the fall of man, but not in diplomacy.

More fatal and completer, though different, was the breach between the commercial bourgeoisie and its politicians. It twitted them, not as the Legitimists did theirs, with having apostatized from their principle, but, on the contrary, with adhering to principles that had become useless.

I have already indicated that, since the entry of Fould in the Ministry, that portion of the commercial bourgeoisie that had enjoyed the lion's share in Louis Philippe's reign, to-wit, the aristocracy of finance, had become Bonapartist. Fould not only represented Bonaparte's interests at the Bourse, he repreesnted also the interests of the Bourse with Bonaparte. A passage from the London "Economist," the European organ of the aristocracy of finance, described most strikingly the attitude of this class. In its issue of February 1, 1851, its Paris correspondent writes: "Now we have it stated from numerous quarters that France wishes above all things for repose. The President declares it in his message to the Legislative Assembly; it is echoed from

---

[1] An allusion to the lilies of the Bourbon coat-of-arms.

the tribune; it is asserted in the journals; it is announced from the pulpit; it is demonstrated by the sensitiveness of the public funds at the least prospect of disturbance, and their firmness the instant it is made manifest that the Executive is far superior in wisdom and power to the factious ex-officials of all former governments."

In its issue of November 29, 1851, the "Economist" declares editorially: "The President is now recognized as the guardian of order on every Stock Exchange of Europe." Accordingly, the *Aristocracy of Finance* condemned the parliamentary strife of the party of Order with the Executive as a "disturbance of order," and hailed every victory of the President over its reputed representatives as a "victory of order." Under "aristocracy of finance" must not, however, be understood merely the large bond negotiators and speculators in government securities, of whom it may be readily understood that their interests and the interests of the Government coincide. The whole modern money trade, the whole banking industry, is most intimately interwoven with the public credit. Part of their business capital requires to be invested in interest-bearing government securities that are promptly convertible into money; their deposits, *i. e.,* the capital placed at their disposal and by them distributed among merchants and industrial establishments, flow partly out of the dividends on government securities. The whole money market, together with the priests of this market, is part and parcel of this "aristocracy of finance" at every epoch when the stability of the government is to them synonymous with "Moses and his prophets." This is so even before things have reached the present stage when every deluge threatens to carry away the old governments themselves.

But the *Industrial Bourgeoisie* also, in its fanaticism for order, was annoyed at the quarrels of the Parliamentary party of Order with the Executive. Thiers, Anglas, Sainte Beuve, etc., received, after their vote of January 18, on the occasion of the discharge of Changarnier, public reprimands from their constituencies, located in the industrial districts, branding their coalition with the Mountain as an act of high treason to the cause of order. Although, true enough, the boastful, vexatious and petty intrigues, through which the struggle of the party of Order with the President manifested itself, deserved no better reception, yet notwithstanding, this bourgeois party, that expects of its representatives to allow the military power to pass without resistance out of the hands of their own Parliament into those of an adventurous Pretender, is not worth even the intrigues that were wasted in its behalf. It showed that the struggle for the maintenance of their public interests, of their class interests, of their political power only incommoded and displeased them, as a disturbance of their private business.

The bourgeois dignitaries of the provincial towns, the magistrates, commercial judges, etc., with hardly any exception, received Bonaparte everywhere on his excursions in the most servile manner, even when, as in Dijon, he attacked the National Assembly and especially the party of Order without reserve.

Business being brisk, as still at the beginning of 1851, the commercial bourgeoisie stormed against every Parliamentary strife, lest business be put out of temper. Business being dull, as from the end of February, 1851, on, the bourgeoisie accused the Parliamentary strifes as the cause of the stand-still, and clamored for quiet in order that business may revive. The debates on revision fell just in the bad times. Seeing the question now was the to be or not to be of the existing form of government, the bourgeoisie felt itself all the more justified in demanding of its Representatives that they put an end to this tormenting provisional status, and preserve the "status quo." This was no contradiction. By putting an end to the provisional status, it understood its continuance, the indefinite putting off of the moment when a final decision had to be arrived at. The "status quo" could be preserved in only one of two ways: either by the prolongation of Bonaparte's term of office or by his constitutional withdrawal and the election of Cavaignac. A part of the bourgeoisie preferred the latter solution, and knew no better advice to give their Representatives than to be silent, to avoid the burning point. If their Representatives did not speak, so argued they, Bonaparte would not act. They desired an ostrich Parliament that would hide its head, in order not to be seen. Another part of the bourgeoisie preferred that Bonaparte, being once in the Presidential chair, be left in the Presidential chair, in order that everything might continue to run in the old ruts. They felt indignant that their

Parliament did not openly break the Constitution and resign without further ado.

The General Councils of the Departments, these provisional representative bodies of the large bourgeoisie, who had adjourned during the vacation of the National Assembly since August 25, pronounced almost unanimously for revision, that is to say, against the Parliament and for Bonaparte.

Still more unequivocally than in its falling out with its Parliamentary Representatives, did the bourgeoisie exhibit its wrath at its literary Representatives, its own press. The verdicts of the bourgeois juries, inflicting excessive fines and shameless sentences of imprisonment for every attack of the bourgeois press upon the usurping aspirations of Bonaparte, for every attempt of the press to defend the political rights of the bourgeoisie against the Executive power, threw, not France alone, but all Europe into amazement.

While on the one hand, as I have indicated, the Parliamentary party of Order ordered itself to keep the peace by screaming for peace; and while it pronounced the political rule of the bourgeoisie irreconciliable with the safety and the existence of the bourgeoisie, by destroying with its own hands in its struggle with the other classes of society all the conditions for its own, the Parliamentary régime; on the other hand, the mass of the bourgeoisie, outside of the Parliament, urged Bonaparte—by its servility towards the President, by its insults to the Parliament, by the brutal treatment of its own press—to suppress and annihilate its speaking and writing organs, its politicians and its literati, its orators' tribune and its press, to the end that, under the protection of a strong and unhampered Government, it might ply its own private pursuits in safety. It declared unmistakably that it longed to be rid of its own political rule, in order to escape the troubles and dangers of ruling.

And this bourgeoisie, that had rebelled against even the Parliamentary and literary contest for the supremacy of its own class, that had betrayed its leaders in this contest, it now has the effrontery to blame the proletariat for not having risen in its defence in a bloody struggle, in a struggle for life! Those bourgeois, who at every turn sacrificed their common class interests to narrow and dirty private interests, and who demanded a similar sacrifice from their own Representatives, now whine that the proletariat has sacrificed their ideal-political to its own material interests! This bourgeois class now strikes the attitude of a pure soul, misunderstood and abandoned, at a critical moment, by the proletariat, that has been misled by the Socialists. And its cry finds a general echo in the bourgeois world. Of course, I do not refer to German cross-road politicians and kindred blockheads. I refer, for instance, to the "Economist," which, as late as November 29, 1851, that is to say, four days before the "coup d'état" pronounced Bonaparte the "Guardian of Order" and Thiers and Berryer "Anarchists," and as early as December 27, 1851, after Bonaparte had silenced those very Anarchists, cries out about the treason committed by "the ignorant, untrained and stupid proletaires against the skill, knowledge, discipline, mental influence, intellectual resources and

moral weight of the middle and upper ranks."
The stupid, ignorant and contemptible mass was
none other than the bourgeoisie itself.

France had, indeed, experienced a sort of commercial crisis in 1851. At the end of February,
there was a falling off of exports as compared
with 1850; in March, business languished and
factories shut down; in April, the condition of
the industrial departments seemed as desperate
as after the February days; in May, business did
not yet pick up; as late as June 28, the reports of
the Bank of France revealed through a tremendous increase of deposits and an equal de-
crease of loans on exchange notes, the standstill
of production; not until the middle of October
did a steady improvement of business set in. The
French bourgeoisie accounted for this stagnation
of business with purely political reasons; it im-
puted the dull times to the strife between the Parliament and the Executive power, to the uncer-
tainty of a provisional form of government, to
the alarming prospects of May 2, 1852. I shall
not deny that all these causes did depress some
branches of industry in Paris and in the Departments. At any rate, this effect of political
circumstances was only local and trifling. Is
there any other proof needed than that the improvement in business set in at the very time
when the political situation was growing worse,
when the political horizon was growing darker,
and when at every moment a stroke of lightning
was expected out of the Elysée—in the middle of
October? The French bourgeois, whose "skill,
knowledge, mental influence and intellectual resources," reach no further than his nose, could,

moreover, during the whole period of the Industrial Exposition in London, have struck with his nose the cause of his own business misery. At the same time that, in France, the factories were being closed, commercial failures broke out in England. While the industrial panic reached its height during April and May in France, in England the commercial panic reached its height in April and May. The same as the French, the English woolen industries suffered, and, as the French, so did the English silk manufacture. Though the English cotton factories went on working, it, nevertheless, was not with the same old profit of 1849 and 1850. The only difference was this: that in France, the crisis was an industrial, in England it was a commercial one; that while in France the factories stood still, they spread themselves in England, but under less favorable circumstances than they had done the years just previous; that, in France, the export, in England, the import trade suffered the heaviest blows. The common cause, which, as a matter of fact, is not to be looked for within the bounds of the French political horizon, was obvious. The years 1849 and 1850 were years of the greatest material prosperity, and of an overproduction that did not manifest itself until 1851. This was especially promoted at the beginning of 1851 by the prospect of the Industrial Exposition; and, as special causes, there were added, first, the failure of the cotton crop of 1850 and 1851; second, the certainty of a larger cotton crop than was expected: first, the rise, then the sudden drop; in short, the oscillations of the cotton market. The crop of raw silk in France had been below the average. Finally, the manufacture of woolen goods had received such an increment since 1849, that the production of wool could not keep step with it, and the price of the raw material rose greatly out of proportion to the price of the manufactured goods. Accordingly, we have here in the raw material of three staple articles a threefold material for a commercial crisis. Apart from these special circumstances, the seeming crisis of the year 1851 was, after all, nothing but the halt that overproduction and overspeculation make regularly in the course of the industrial cycle, before pulling all their forces together in order to rush feverishly over the last stretch, and arrive again at their point of departure—the *General Commercial Crisis*. At such intervals in the history of trade, commercial failures break out in England, while, in France, industry itself is stopped, partly because it is compelled to retreat through the competition of the English, that, at such times becomes resistless in all markets, and partly because, as an industry of luxuries, it is affected with preference by every stoppage of trade. Thus, besides the general crisis, France experiences her own national crises, which, however, are determined by and conditioned upon the general state of the world's market much more than by local French influences. It will not be devoid of interest to contrast the prejudgment of the French bourgeois with the judgment of the English bourgeois. One of the largest Liverpool firms writes in its yearly report of trade for 1851: "Few years have more completely disappointed the expectations entertained at their beginning than the year that has just passed; instead of the great prosperity, that was unanimously looked forward to, it proved itself one of the most discouraging years during the last quarter of a century. This applies, of course, only to the mercantile, not to the industrial classes. And yet, surely there were grounds at the beginning of the year from which to draw a contrary conclusion; the stock of products was scanty, capital was abundant, provisions cheap, a rich autumn was assured, there was uninterrupted peace on the continent and no political and financial disturbances at home; indeed, never were the wings of trade more unshackled. . . What is this unfavorable result to be ascribed to? We believe to excessive trade in imports as well as exports. If our merchants do not themselves rein in their activity, nothing can keep us going, except a panic every three years."

Imagine now the French bourgeois, in the midst of this business panic, having his trade-sick brain tortured, buzzed at and deafened with rumors of a "coup d'état" and the restoration of universal suffrage; with the struggle between the Legislature and the Executive; with the Fronde warfare between Orleanists and Legitimists; with communistic conspiracies in southern France; wth alleged Jacqueries[2] in the Departments of Nièvre and Cher; with the advertisements of the several candidates for President; with "social solutions" huckstered about by the journals; with the threats of the republicans to uphold, arms in hand, the Constitution and universal suffrage;

---

[2] Peasant revolts.

with the gospels, according to the emigrant heroes "in partibus," who announced the destruction of the world for May 2,—imagine that, and one can understand how the bourgeois, in this unspeakable and noisy confusion of fusion, revision, prorogation, constitution, conspiracy, coalition, emigration, usurpation and revolution, blurts out at his parliamentary republic: *"Rather an End With Fright, Than a Fright Without End."*

Bonaparte understood this cry. His perspicacity was sharpened by the growing anxiety of the creditors' class, who, with every sunset, that brought nearer the day of payment, the 2d of May, 1852, saw in the motion of the stars a protest against their earthly drafts. They had become regular astrologers The National Assembly had cut off Bonaparte's hope of a constitutional prolongation of his term; the candidature of the Prince of Joinville tolerated no further vacillation.

If ever an event cast its shadow before it long before its occurrence, it was Bonaparte's "coup d'état." Already on January 29, 1849, barely a month after his election, he had made to Changarnier a proposition to that effect. His own Prime Minister, Odillon Barrot, had covertly, in 1849, and Thiers openly, in the winter of 1850, revealed the scheme of the "coup d'état." In May, 1851, Persigny had again sought to win Changarnier over to the "coup," and the "Messager de l'Assemblée" newspaper had published this conversation. At every parliamentary storm, the Bonapartist papers threatened a "coup," and the nearer the

crisis approached, all the louder grew their
tone. At the orgies, that Bonaparte celebrated
every night with a swell mob of males and
females, every time the hour of midnight drew
nigh and plenteous libations had loosened the
tongues and heated the minds of the revelers,
the "coup" was resolved upon for the next
morning. Swords were then drawn, glasses
clinked, the Representatives were thrown out
at the windows, the imperial mantle fell upon
the shoulders of Bonaparte, until the next
morning again drove away the spook, and
astonished Paris learned, from not very reserved Vestals and indiscreet Paladins, the
danger it had once more escaped. During the
months of September and October, the rumors
of a "coup d'état" tumbled close upon one another's heels. At the same time the shadow
gathered color, like a confused daguerreotype.
Follow the issues of the European daily press
for the months of September and October, and
items like this will be found literally:

"Rumors of a 'coup' fill Paris. The capital,
it is said, is to be filled with troops by night,
and the next morning decrees are to be issued
dissolving the National Assembly, placing the
Department of the Seine in state of siege, restoring universal suffrage, and appealing to
the people. Bonaparte is rumored to be looking for Ministers to execute these illegal decrees."

The newspaper correspondence that brought
this news always close ominously with "postponed." The "coup" was ever the fixed idea
of Bonaparte. With this idea he had stepped

again upon French soil. It had such full pos
session of him that he was constantly betray
ing and blabbing it out. He was so weak tha
he was as constantly giving it up again. The
shadow of the "coup" had become so familiar
a spectre to the Parisians, that they refused to
believe it when it finally did appear in flesl
and blood. Consequently, it was neither the
reticent backwardness of the chief of the "So
ciety of December 10," nor an unthought o
surprise of the National Assembly that causec
the success of the "coup." When it succeeded
it did so despite his indiscretion and with it:
anticipation—a necessary, unavoidable resul
of the development that had preceded.

On October 10, Bonaparte announced to hi:
Ministers his decision to restore universal suf
frage; on the 16th day they handed in thei
resignations; on the 26th Paris learned of the
formation of the Thorigny Ministry. The Pre
fect of Police, Carlier, was simultaneously re
placed by Maupas; and the chief of the Firs
Military Division Magnan, concentrated the
most reliable regiments in the capital. On No
vember 4, the National Assembly re-opened it:
sessions. There was nothing left for it to dc
but to repeat, in short recapitulation, the
course it had traversed, and to prove that i
had been buried only after it had expired.

The first post that it had forfeited in the
struggle with the Executive was the Ministry
It had solemnly to admit this loss by accept
ing as genuine the Thorigny Ministry, which
was but a pretence. The permanent Commit
tee had received Mr. Giraud with laughter

when he introduced himself in the name of the new Ministers. So weak a Ministry for so strong a measure as the restoration of universal suffrage! The question, however, then was to do nothing *in,* everything *against* the parliament.

On the very day of its re-opening, the National Assembly received the message from Bonaparte demanding the restoration of universal suffrage and the repeal of the law of May 31, 1850. On the same day, his Ministers introduced a decree to that effect. The Assembly promptly rejected the motion of urgency made by the Ministers, but repealed the law itself, on November 13, by a vote of 355 against 348. Thus it once more tore to pieces its own mandate, once more certified to the fact that it had transformed itself from a freely chosen representative body of the nation into the usurpatory parliament of a class; it once more admitted that it had itself severed the muscles that connected the parliamentary head with the body of the nation.

While the Executive power appealed from the National Assembly to the people by its motion for the restoration of universal suffrage, the Legislative power appealed from the people to the Army by its "Quæstors' Bill." This bill was to establish its right to immediate requisitions for troops, to build up a parliamentary army. By thus appointing the Army umpire between itself and the people, between itself and Bonaparte; by thus recognizing the Army as the decisive power in the State, the National Assembly was constrained to admit that it had long given up all claim to supremacy. By debating the right to make requisitions for troops, instead of forthwith collecting them, it betrayed its own doubts touching its own power. By subsequently rejecting the "Quæstors' Bill," it publicly confessed its impotence. This bill fell through with a minority of 108 votes; the Mountain had, accordingly, thrown the casting vote. It now found itself in the predicament of Buridan's donkey, not, indeed, between two sacks of hay, forced to decide which of the two was the more attractive, but between two showers of blows, forced to decide which of the two was the harder; fear of Changarnier, on one side, fear of Bonaparte, on the other. It must be admitted the position was not a heroic one.

On November 18, an amendment was moved to the Act, passed by the party of Order, on municipal elections to the effect that, instead of three years, a domicile of one year should suffice. The amendment was lost by a single vote—but this vote, it soon transpired, was a mistake. Owing to the divisions within its own hostile factions, the party of Order had long since forfeited its independent parliamentary majority. It was now plain that there was no longer any majority in the parliament. The National Assembly had become impotent even to decide. Its atomic parts were no longer held together by any cohesive power; it had expended its last breath, it was dead.

Finally, the mass of the bourgeoisie outside of the parliament was once more solemnly to confirm its rupture with the bourgeoisie inside of the parliament a few days before the catastrophe. Thiers, as a parliamentary hero conspicuously smitten by that incurable disease—Parliamentary Idiocy—, had hatched out jointly with the Council of State, after the death of the parliament, a new parliamentary intrigue in the shape of a "Responsibility Law," that was intended to lock up the President within the walls of the Constitution. The same as, on Sepember 15, Bonaparte bewitched the fishwives, like a second Massaniello, on the occasion of laying the corner-stone for the Market of Paris,—though, it must be admitted, one fishwife was equal to seventeen Burgraves in real power—; the same as, after the introduction of the "Quæstors' Bill," he enthused the lieutenants, who were being treated at the Elysée;—so, likewise, did he now, on November 25, carry away with him the industrial bourgeoisie, assembled at the Circus, to receive from his hands the prize-medals that had been awarded at the London Industrial Exposition. I here reproduce the typical part of his speech, from the "Journal des Débats":

"With such unhoped for successes, I am justified to repeat how great the French republic would be if she were only allowed to pursue her real interests, and reform her institutions, instead of being constantly disturbed in this by demagogues, on one side, and, on the other, by monarchic hallucinations. (Loud, stormy and continued applause from all parts of the amphitheater). The monarchic hallucinations hamper all progress and all serious departments of industry. Instead of progress, we have struggle only. Men, formerly the most zealous supporters of royal authority and prerogative, become the partisans of a convention that has no purpose other than to weaken an authority that is born of universal suffrage. (Loud and prolonged applause). We see men, who have suffered most from the revolution and complained bitterest of it, provoking a new one for the sole purpose of putting fetters on the will of the nation. . . . I promise you peace for the future." (Bravo! Bravo! Stormy bravos.)

Thus the industrial bourgeoisie shouts its servile "Bravo!" to the "coup d'état" of December 2, to the destruction of the parliament, to the downfall of their own reign, to the dictatorship of Bonaparte. The rear of the applause of November 25 was responded to by the roar of cannon on December 4, and the house of Mr. Sallandrouze, who had been loudest in applauding, was the one demolished by most of the bombs.

Cromwell, when he dissolved the Long Parliament, walked alone into its midst, pulled out his watch in order that the body should not continue to exist one minute beyond the term fixed for it by him, and drove out each individual member with gay and humorous invectives. Napoleon, smaller than his prototype, at least went on the 18th Brumaire into the legislative body, and, though in a tremulous voice, read to it its sentence of death. The second Bonaparte, who, moreover, found himself in possession of an executive power very different from that of either Cromwell

or Napoleon, did not look for his model in the
annals of universal history, but in the annals
of the "Society of December 10," in the annals of criminal jurisprudence. He robs the
Bank of France of twenty-five million francs;
buys General Magnan with one million and
the soldiers with fifteen francs and a drink to
each; comes secretly together with his accom-
plices like a thief by night; has the houses of
the most dangerous leaders in the parliament
broken into; Cavaignac, Lamorcière, Leflô,
Changarnier, Charras, Thiers, Baze, etc., taken
out of their beds; the principal places of
Paris, the building of the parliament included,
occupied with troops; and, early the next
morning, loud-sounding placards posted on all
the walls proclaiming the dissolution of the
National Assembly and of the Council of
State, the restoration of universal suffrage,
and the placing of the Department of the
Seine under the state of siege. In the same
way he shortly after sneaked into the "Moniteur" a false document, according to which in-
fluential parliamentary names had grouped
themselves round him in a Committee of the
Nation.

Amidst cries of "Long live the Republic!",
the rump-parliament, assembled at the Mayor's
building of the Tenth Arrondissement, and
composed mainly of Legitimists and Orleanists, resolves to depose Bonaparte; it harangues in vain the gaping mass gathered before
the building, and is finally dragged first, under
the escort of African sharpshooters, to the
barracks of Orsay, and then bundled into con-

victs' wagons and transported to the prisons of Mazas, Ham and Vincennes. Thus ended the party of Order, the Legislative Assembly and the February revolution.

Before hastening to the end, let us sum up shortly the plan of its history:

I.—*First Period.* From February 24 to May 4, 1848. February period. Prologue. Universal fraternity swindle.

II.—*Second Period.* Period in which the republic is constituted, and of the Constitutive National Assembly.

    1. May 4 to June 25, 1848. Struggle of all the classes against the proletariat. Defeat of the proletariat in the June days.

    2. June 25 to December 10, 1848. Dictatorship of the pure bourgeois republicans. Drafting of the Constitution. The state of siege hangs over Paris. The bourgeois dictatorship set aside on December 10 by the election of Bonaparte as President.

    3. December 20, 1848, to May 20, 1849. Struggle of the Constitutive Assembly with Bonaparte and with the united party of Order. Death of the Constitutive Assembly. Downfall of the republican bourgeoisie.

III.—*Third Period.* Period of the constitutional republic and of the Legislative National Assembly.

    1. May 29 to June 13, 1849. Struggle of the small traders', middle class with the bourgeoisie and with Bonaparte. Defeat of the small traders' democracy.

    2. June 13, 1849, to May, 1850. Parliamentary dictatorship of the party of Order. Completes its reign by the abolition of universal suffrage, but loses the parliamentary Ministry.

    3. May 31, 1850, to December 2, 1851. Struggle between the parliamentary bourgeoisie and Bonaparte.

      a. May 31, 1850, to January 12, 1851. The

parliament loses the supreme command over the Army.

b. January 12 to April 11, 1851. The parliament succumbs in the attempts to regain possession of the administrative power. The party of Order loses its independent parliamentary majority. Its coalition with the republicans and the Mountain.

c. April 11 to October 9, 1851. Attempts at revision, fusion and prorogation. The party of Order dissolves into its component parts. The breach between the bourgeois parliament and the bourgeois press, on the one hand, and the bourgeois mass, on the other, becomes permanent.

d. October 9 to December 2, 1851. Open breach between the parliament and the executive power. It draws up its own decree of death, and goes under, left in the lurch by its own class, by the Army, and by all the other classes. Downfall of the parliamentary régime and of the reign of the bourgeoisie. Bonaparte's triumph. Parody of the imperialist restoration.

VII.

The *Social Republic* appeared as a mere phrase, as a prophecy on the threshold of the February Revolution; it was smothered in the blood of the Parisian proletariat during the days of 1848; but it stalks about as a spectre throughout the following acts of the drama. The *Democratic* Republic next makes its bow; it goes out in a fizzle on June 13, 1849, with its runaway small traders; but, on fleeing, it scatters behind it all the more bragging announcements of what it means do to. The *Parliamentary Republic*, together with the bourgeoisie, then appropriates the whole stage; it lives its life to the full extent of its being; but the 2d of December, 1851, buries it under the terror-stricken cry of the allied royalists: "Long live the Republic!"

The French bourgeoisie reared up against the reign of the working proletariat;—it brought to power the slum-proletariat, with the chief of the "Society of December 10" at its head. It kept France in breathless fear over the prospective terror of "red anarchy;"—Bonaparte discounted the prospect when, on December 4, he had the leading citizens of the Boulevard Montmartre and the Boulevard des Italiens shot down from their windows by the grog-inspired "Army of Order." It made the apotheosis of the sabre;—now the sabre rules it. It destroyed the revolutionary press;—now its own press is annihilated. It placed public meetings under police surveillance;—now its own salons are subject to police inspection. It disbanded the democratic National Guards;—now its own National Guard is disbanded. It instituted the state of siege;—now itself is made subject thereto. It supplanted the jury by military commissions;—now military commissions supplant its own juries. It subjected the education of the people to the parsons' interests;—the parsons' interests now subject it to their own systems. It ordered transportations without trial;—now itself is transported without trial. It suppressed every movement of society with physical force;—now every movement of its own class is suppressed by physical force. Out of enthusiasm for the gold bag, it rebelled against its own political leaders and writers;—now, its political leaders and writers are set aside, but the gold bag is plundered, after

the mouth of the bourgeoisie has been gagged
and its pen broken. The bourgeoisie tirelessly
shouted to the revolution, in the language of St.
Orsenius to the Christians: "Fuge, Tace,
Quiesce!"—flee, be silent, submit!—; Bonaparte
shouts to the bourgeoisie: "Fuge, Tace,
Quiesce!"—flee, be silent, submit!

The French bourgeoisie had long since solved
Napoleon's dilemma: "Dans cinquante ans l'Europe sera républicaine ou cosaque."[1] , It found
the solution in the république cosaque."[2] No
Circe distorted with wicked charms the work
of art of the bourgeois republic into a monstros-
ity. That republic lost nothing but the appearance of decency. The France of to-day was
ready-made within the womb of the Parliamentary republic. All that was wanted was a bayonet thrust, in order that the bubble burst, and
the monster leap forth to sight.

Why did not the Parisian proletariat rise after
the 2d of December?

The downfall of the bourgeoisie was as yet
merely decreed; the decree was not yet executed.
Any earnest uprising of the proletariat would
have forthwith revived this bourgeoisie, would
have brought on its reconciliation with the army,
and would have insured a second June rout to
the workingmen.

On December 4, the proletariat was incited to
fight by Messrs. Bourgeois & Small-Trader. On
the evening of that day, several legions of the National Guard promised to appear armed and uni-

---

[1] Within fifty years Europe will be either republican or
Cossack.
[2] Cossack republic.

formed on the place of battle. This arose from
the circumstance that Messrs. Bourgeois & Small-
Trader had got wind that, in one of his decrees
of December 2, Bonaparte abolished the secret
ballot, and ordered them to enter the words
"Yes" and "No" after their names in the official register. Bonaparte took alarm at the
stand taken on December 4. During the night
he caused placards to be posted on all the street
corners of Paris, announcing the restoration of
the secret ballot. Messrs. Bourgeois & Small-
Trader believed they had gained their point. The
absentees, the next morning, were Messieurs.
Bourgeois & Small-Trader.

During the night of December 1 and 2, the
Parisian proletariat was robbed of its leaders and
chiefs of barricades by a raid of Bonaparte's.
An army without officers, disinclined by the recollections of June, 1848 and 1849, and May, 1850,
to fight under the banner of the Montagnards, it
left to its vanguard, the secret societies, the work
of saving the insurrectionary honor of Paris,
which the bourgeoisie had yielded to the soldiery
so submissvely that Bonaparte was later justified in disarming the National Guard upon the
scornful ground that he feared their arms would
be used against themselves by the Anarchists!

"C'est le triomphe complet et definitif du Socialism!"[3]   Thus did Guizot characterize the
2d of December. But, although the downfall
of the parliamentary republic carries with it the
germ of the triumph of the proletarian revolution, its immediate and tangible result was the
triumph of Bonaparte over the parliament. of

[3] It is the complete and definite triumph of Socialism.

the Executive over the Legislative power, of force
without phrases over the force of phrases. In
the parliament, the nation raised its collective
will to the dignity of law, *i. e.*, it raised the
law of the ruling class to the dignity of its collective will. Before the Executive power, the
nation abdicates all will of its own, and submits
to the orders of an outsider of Authority. In
contrast with the Legislative, the Executive power expresses the heteronomy of the nation in
contrast with its autonomy. Accordingly,
France seems to have escaped the despotism of
a class only in order to fall under the despotism
of an individual, under the authority, at that,
of an individual without authority. The struggle seems to settle down to the point where all
classes drop down on their knees, equally impotent and equally dumb.

All the same, the revolution is thoroughgoing.
It still is on its passage through purgatory. It
does its work methodically. Down to December
2, 1851, it had fulfilled one-half of its programme;
it now fulfils the other half. It first ripens the
power of the Legislature into fullest maturity
in order to be able to overthrow it. Now that it
has accomplished that, the revolution proceeds
to ripen the power of the Executive into equal
maturity; it reduces this power to its purest
expression; isolates it; places it before itself
as the sole subject for reproof in order to concentrate against it all the revolutionary forces
of destruction. When the revolution shall have
accomplished this second part of its preliminary
programme, Europe will jump up from her seat

to exclaim: "Well hast thou grubbed, old mole!"

The Executive power, with its tremendous bureaucratic and military organization; with its wide-spreading and artificial machinery of government—an army of office-holders, half a million strong, together with a military force of another million men—; this fearful body of parasites, that coils itself like a snake around French society, stopping all its pores, originated at the time of the absolute monarchy, along with the decline of feudalism, which it helped to hasten. The princely privileges of the landed proprietors and cities were transformed into so many attributes of the Executive power; the feudal dignitaries into paid office-holders: and the confusing design of conflicting mediæval seigniories, into the well regulated plan of a government, work is subdivided and centralized as in the factory. The first French revolution, having as a mission to sweep away all local, territorial, urban and provincial special privileges, with the object of establishing the civic unity of the nation, was bound to develop what the absolute monarchy had begun—the work of centralization, together with the range, the attributes and the menials of government. Napoleon completed this governmental machinery. The Legitimist and the July Monarchy contribute nothing thereto, except a greater subdivision of labor, that grew in the same measure as the division and subdivision of labor within bourgeois society raised new groups and interests, i. e., new material for the administration of government. Each *Common* interest was in turn forthwith removed from society, set up against it as a higher *Collective* interest, wrested from the individual activity of the members of society, and turned into a subject for governmental administration, —from the bridges, the school house and the communal property of a village community, up to the railroads, the national wealth and the national University of France. Finally, the parliamentary republic found itself, in its struggle against the revolution, compelled, with its repressive measures, to strengthen the means and the centralization of the government. Each overturn, instead of breaking up, carried this machine to higher perfection. The parties, that alternately wrestled for supremacy, looked upon the possession of this tremendous governmental structure as the principal spoils of their victory.

Nevertheless, under the absolute monarchy, during the first revolution, and under Napoleon, the bureaucracy was only the means whereby to prepare the class rule of the bourgeoisie; under the restoration, under Louis Philippe, and under the parliamentary republic, it was the instrument of the ruling class, however eagerly this class strained after autocracy. Not before the advent of the second Bonaparte does the government seem to have made itself fully independent. The machinery of government has by this time so thoroughly fortified itself against society, that the chief of the "Society of December 10" is thought good enough to be at its head; a fortune-hunter, run in from abroad, is raised on its shield by a drunken soldiery, bought by himself with liquor and sausages, and whom he is forced ever again to throw sops to. Hence

the timid despair, the sense of crushing humiliation and degradation that oppresses the breast of
France and makes her to choke. She feels dis-
honored.

And yet the French Government does not
float in the air. Bonaparte represents an economic class, and that the most numerous in the
commonweal of France—the *Allotment Farmer.*"*

As the Bourbons are the dynasty of large landed property, as the Orleans are the dynasty of
money, so are the Bonapartes the dynasty of the
farmer. *i. e.*, of the French masses. Not the
Bonaparte, who threw himself at the feet of the
bourgeois parliament, but the Bonaparte, who
swept away the bourgeois parliament, is the elect
of this farmer class. For three years the cities
had succeeded in falsifying the meaning of the
election of December 10, and in cheating the
farmer out of the restoration of the Empire.
The election of December 10, 1848, is not carried out until the "coup d'état" of December 2,
1851.

The allotment farmers are an immense mass,
whose individual members live in identical conditions, without, however, entering into manifold
relations with one another. Their method of
production isolates them from one another, instead of drawing them into mutual intercourse.
This isolation is promoted by the poor means of
communication in France, together with the poverty of the farmers themselves. Their field of
production, the small allotment of land that each

* The first French Revolution distributed the bulk of the
territory of France, held at the time by the feudal lords, in
small patches among the cultivators of the soil. This allotment of lands created the French farmer class.

cultivates, allows no room for a division of labor, and no opportunity for the application of science; in other words, it shuts out manifoldness of development, diversity of talent, and the luxury of social relations. Every single farmer family is almost self-sufficient; itself produces directly the greater part of what it consumes; and it earns its livelihood more by means of an interchange with nature than by intercourse with society. We have the allotted patch of land, the farmer and his family; alongside of that another allotted patch of land, another farmer and another family. A bunch of these makes up a village; a bunch of villages makes up a Department. Thus the large mass of the French nation is constituted by the simple addition of equal magnitudes—much as a bag with potatoes constitutes a potato-bag. In so far as millions of families live under economic conditons that separate their mode of life, their interests and their culture from those of the other classes, and that place them in an attitude hostile toward the latter, they constitute a class; in so far as there exists only a local connection among these farmers, a connection which the individuality and exclusiveness of their interests prevent from generating among them any unity of interest, national connections, and political organization, they do not constitute a class. Consequently, they are unable to assert their class interests in their own name, be it by a parliament or by convention. They can not represent one another, they must themselves be represented. Their representative must at the same time appear as their master, as an authority over them, as an unlimited governmental power, that protects them from above, bestows rain and sunshine upon them. Accordingly, the political influence of the allotment farmer finds its ultimate expression in an Executive power that subjugates the commonweal to its own autocratic will.

Historic tradition has given birth to the superstition among the French farmers that a man named Napoleon would restore to them all manner of glory. Now, then, an individual turns up, who gives himself out as that man because, obedient to the "Code Napoléon," which provides that "La récherche de la paternité est interdite,"[5] he carries the name of Napoleon.[6] After a vagabondage of twenty years, and a series of grotesque adventures, the myth is verified, and that man becomes the Emperor of the French. The rooted thought of the Nephew becomes a reality because it coincided with the rooted thought of the most numerous class among the French.

"But," I shall be objected to, "what about the farmers' uprisings over half France, the raids of the Army upon the farmers, the wholesale imprisonment and transportation of farmers?"

Indeed, since Louis XIV., France has not experienced such persecutions of the farmer on the ground of his demagogic machinations."

But this should be well understood: The Bonaparte dynasty does not represent the revolutionary, it represents the conservative farmer; it does not represent the farmer, who presses beyond his own economic conditions, his little allot-

_____

[5] The inquiry into paternity is forbidden.
[6] L. N. Bonaparte is said to have been an illegitimate son.

ment of land, it represents him rather who would confirm these conditions; it does not represent the rural population, that, thanks to its own inherent energy, wishes, jointly with the cities to overthrow the old order, it represents, on the contrary, the rural population that, hide-bound in the old order, seeks to see itself, together with its allotments, saved and favored by the ghost of the Empire; it represents, not the intelligence, but the superstition of the farmer; not his judgment, but his bias; not his future, but his past; not his modern Cevennes;[7] but his modern Vendée.[8]

The three years' severe rule of the parliamentary republic had freed a part of the French farmers from the Napoleonic illusion, and, though even only superficially; had revolutionized them. The bourgeoisie threw them, however, violently back every time that they set themselves in motion. Under the parliamentary republic, the modern wrestled with the traditional consciousness of the French farmer. The process went on in the form of a continuous struggle between the school teachers and the parsons;— the bourgeoisie knocked the school teachers down. For the first time, the farmer made an effort to take an independent stand in the government of the country; this manifested itself in the prolonged conflicts of the Mayors with the Prefects;—the bourgeoisie deposed the Mayors. Finally, during the period of the parliamentary republic, the farmers of several localities rose

[7] The Cevennes were the theater of the most numerous revolutionary uprisings of the farmer class.

[8] La Vendée was the theater of protracted reactionary uprisings of the farmer class under the first Revolution.

against their own product, the Army;—the bourgeoisie punished them with states of siege and executions. And this is the identical bourgeoisie, that now howls over the "stupidity of the masses," over the "vile multitude," which, it claims, betrayed it to Bonaparte. Itself has violently fortified the imperialism of the farmer class; it firmly maintained the conditions that constitute the birth-place of this farmer-religion. Indeed, the bourgeoisie has every reason to fear the stupidity of the masses—so long as they remain conservative; and their intelligence—so soon as they become revolutionary.

In the revolts that took place after the "coup d'état" a part of the French farmers protested, arms in hand, against their own vote of December 10, 1848. The school house had, since 1848, sharpened their wits. But they had bound themselves over to the nether world of history, and history kept them to their word. Moreover, the majority of this population was still so full of prejudices that, just in the "reddest" Departments, it voted openly for Bonaparte. The National Assembly prevented, as it thought, this population from walking; the farmers now snapped the fetters which the cities had struck upon the will of the country districts. In some places they even indulged the grotesque hallucination of a "Convention together with a Napoleon."

After the first revolution had converted the serf farmers into freeholders, Napoleon fixed and regulated the conditions under which, unmolested, they could exploit the soil of France, that had just fallen into their hands, and expiate the youthful passion for property. But that which now bears the French farmer down is that very allotment of land; it is the partition of the soil, the form of ownership, which Napoleon had consolidated. These are the material conditions that turned the French feudal peasant into a small or allotment farmer, and Napoleon into an Emperor. Two generations have sufficed to produce the inevitable result: the progressive deterioration of agriculture, and the progressive encumbering of the agriculturist. The "Napoleonic" form of ownership, which, at the beginning of the nineteenth century was the condition for the emancipation and enrichment of the French rural population, has, in the course of the century, developed into the law of their enslavement and pauperism. Now, then, this very law is the first of the "idées Napoléoniennes," which the second Bonaparte must uphold. If he still shares with the farmers the illusion of seeking, not in the system of the small allotment itself, but outside of that system, in the influence of secondary conditions, the cause of their ruin, his experiments are bound to burst like soap-bubbles against the modern system of production.

The economic development of the allotment system has turned bottom upward the relation of the farmer to the other classes of society. Under Napoleon, the parceling out of the agricultural lands into small allotments supplemented in the country the free competition and the incipient large production of the cities. The farmer class was the ubiquitous protest against the aristocracy of land, just then overthrown. The roots that the system of small allotments cast into the soil of France, deprived feudalism of all nutriment. Its boundary-posts constituted the natural buttress of the bourgeoisie against every stroke of the old overlords. But in the course of the nineteenth century, the City Usurer stepped into the shoes of the Feudal Lord, the Mortgage substituted the Feudal Duties formerly yielded by the soil, bourgeois Capital took the place of the aristocracy of Landed Property. The former allotments are now only a pretext that allows the capitalist class to draw profit, interest and rent from agricultural lands, and to leave to the farmer himself the task of seeing to it that he knock out his wages. The mortgage indebtedness that burdens the soil of France imposes upon the French farmer class the payment of an interest as great as the annual interest on the whole British national debt. In this slavery of capital, whither its development drives it irresistibly, the allotment system has transformed the mass of the French nation into troglodytes. Sixteen million farmers (women and children included), house in hovels most of which have only one opening, some two, and the few most favored ones three. Windows are to a house what the five senses are to the head. The bourgeois social order, which, at the beginning of the century, placed the State as a sentinel before the newly instituted allotment, and that manured this with laurels, has become a vampire that sucks out its heart-blood and its very brain, and throws it into the alchemist's pot of capital. The "Code Napoleon" is now but the codex of execution, of sheriff's sales and of intensified taxation. To the four million (children, etc., included) official paupers, vagabonds, criminals and prostitutes, that France numbers, must be added five million souls who hover over the precipice of life, and either sojourn in the country itself, or float with their rags and their children from the country to the cities, and from the cities back to the country. Accordingly, the interests of the farmers are no longer, as under Napoleon, in harmony but in conflict with the interests of the bourgeoisie, *i. e.*, with capital; they find their natural allies and leaders among the urban proletariat, whose mission is the overthrow of the bourgeois social order. But the "strong and unlimited government"—and this is the second of the "idées Napoléoniennes," which the second Napoleon has to carry out—, has for its mission the forcible defence of this very "material" social order, a "material order" that furnishes the slogan in Bonaparte's proclamations against the farmers in revolt.

Along with the mortgage, imposed by capital upon the farmer's allotment, this is burdened by taxation. Taxation is the fountain of life to the bureaucracy, the Army, the parsons and the court, in short to the whole apparatus of the Executive power. A strong government, and heavy taxes are identical. The system of ownership, involved in the system of allotments lends itself by nature for the groundwork of a powerful and numerous bureaucracy: it produces an even level of conditions and of persons over the whole surface of the country; it, therefore, allows the exercise of an even influence upon all parts of this even mass from a high central point downwards; it annihilates the aristocratic gradations between the popular masses and the Government; it, consequently, calls from all sides for the direct intervention of the Government and for the intervention of the latter's immediate organs; and, finally, it produces an unemployed excess of population, that finds no room either in the country or in the cities, that, consequently, snatches after public office as a sort of dignified alms, and provokes the creation of further offices. With the new markets, which he opened at the point of the bayonet, and with the plunder of the continent, Napoleon returned to the farmer class with interest the taxes wrung from them. These taxes were then a goad to the industry of the farmer, while now, on the contrary, they rob his industry of its last source of support, and completely sap his power to resist poverty. Indeed, an enormous bureaucracy, richly gallooned and well fed is that "idée Napolénienne" that above all others suits the requirements of the second Bonaparte. How else should it be, seeing he is forced to raise alongside of the actual classes of society, an artificial class, to which the maintenance of his own régime must be a knife-and-fork question? One of his first financial operations was, accordingly, the raising of the salaries of the government employés to their former standard, and the creation of new sinecures.

Another "idée Napoléonienne" is the rule of the parsons as an instrument of government. But while the new-born allotment, in harmony with society, in its dependence upon the powers of nature, and in its subordination to the authority that protected it from above, was naturally religious, the debt-broken allotment, on the con-

trary, at odds with society and authority, and
driven beyond its own narrow bounds, becomes
as naturally irreligious. Heaven was quite a
pretty gift thrown in with the narrow strip of
land that had just been won, all the more as it
makes the weather; it, however, becomes an
insult from the moment it is forced upon the
farmer as a substitute for his allotment. Then
the parson appears merely as the anointed blood-
hound of the earthly police,—yet another "idée
Napoléonienne." The expedition against Rome
will next time take place in France, but in a
reverse sense from that of M. de Montalembert.

Finally, the culminating point of the "idées
Napoléoniennes" is the preponderance of the
Army. The Army was the "point of honor" with
the allotment farmers: it was themselves turned
into masters, defending abroad their newly established property, glorifying their recently conquered nationality, plundering and revolutionizing the world. The uniform was their State cos-
tume; war was their poetry; the allotment, ex-
panded and rounded up in their phantasy, was
the fatherland; and patriotism became the ideal
form of property. But the foe, against whom
the French farmer must now defend his property, are not the Cossacks, they are the sheriffs
and the tax collectors. The allotment no longer
lies in the so-called fatherland, but in the register
of mortgages. The Army itself no longer is
the flower of the youth of the farmers, it is the
swamp-blossom of the slum-proletariat of the
farmer class. It consists of "remplaçants," sub-
stitutes, just as the second Bonaparte himself is
but a remplaçant," a substitute, for Napoleon.

Its feats of heroism are now performed in raids instituted against farmers and in the service of the police;—and when the internal contradictions of his own system shall drive the chief of the "Society of December 10" across the French frontier, that Army will, after a few bandit-raids, gather no laurels but only hard knocks.

It is evident that all the "idées Napoléoniennes" are the ideas of the undeveloped and youthfully fresh allotment; they are an absurdity for the allotment that now survives. They are only the hallucinations of its death struggle: words turned to hollow phrases, spirits turned to spooks. But this parody of the Empire was requisite in order to free the mass of the French nation from the weight of tradition, and to elaborate sharply the contrast between Government and Society. Along with the progressive decay of the allotment, the governmental structure, reared upon it, breaks down. The centralization of Government, required by modern society, rises only upon the ruins of the military and bureaucratic governmental machinery that was forged in contrast to feudalism.

The conditions of the French farmers' class solve to us the riddle of the general elections of December 20 and 21, that led the second Bonaparte to the top of Sinai, not to receive, but to decree laws.

The bourgeoisie had now, manifestly, no choice but to elect Bonaparte. When, at the Council of Constance, the puritans complained of the sinful life of the Popes, and moaned about the need of a reform in morals, Cardinal d'Ailly thundered into their faces: "Only the devil in his own person can now save the Catholic Church, and you demand angels." So, likewise, did the French bourgeoisie cry out after the "coup d'état": "Only the chief of the 'Society of December 10' can now save bourgeois society; only theft can save property, only perjury religion, only bastardy the family, only disorder order!"

Bonaparte, as autocratic Executive power, fulfills his mission to secure "bourgeois order." But the strength of this bourgeois order lies in the middle class. He feels himself the representative of the middle class, and issues his decrees in that sense. Nevertheless, he is something only because he has broken the political power of this class, and daily breaks it anew. Hence he feels himself the adversary of the political and the literary power of the middle class. But, by protecting their material, he nourishes anew their political power. Consequently, the cause must be kept alive, but the result, wherever it manifests itself, swept out of existence. But this procedure is impossible without slight mistakings of causes and effects, seeing that both, in their mutual action and reaction, lose their distinctive marks. Thereupon, new decrees, that blur the line of distinction. Bonaparte, furthermore, feels himself, as against the bourgeoisie, the representative of the farmer and the people in general, who, within bourgeois society, is to render the lower classes of society happy. To this end, new decrees, intended to exploit the "true Socialists," together with their governmental wisdom. But, above all, Bonaparte feels himself the chief of the "Society of December 10," the representative of the slum-proletariat, to which he himself, his immediate surroundings, his Government, and his army alike belong, the main object with all of whom is to be good to themselves, and draw Californian tickets out of the national treasury. And he affirms his chieftainship of the "Society of December 10" with decrees, without decrees, and despite decrees.

This contradictory mission of the man explains the contradictions of his own Government, and that confused groping about, that now seeks to win, then to humiliate now this class and then that, and finishes by arraying against itself all the classes; whose actual insecurity constitutes a highly comical contrast with the imperious, categoric style of the Government acts, copied closely from the Uncle.

Industry and commerce, i. e., the business of the middle class, are to be made to blossom in hot-house style under the "strong Government." Loans for a number of railroad grants. But the Bonapartist slum-proletariat is to enrich itself. Peculation is carried on with railroad concessions on the Bourse by the initiated; but no capital is forthcoming for the railroads. The bank then pledges itself to make advances upon railroad stock; but the bank is itself to be exploited; hence, it must be cajoled; it is released of the obligation to publish its reports weekly. Then follows a leonine treaty between the bank and the Government. The people are to be occupied: public works are ordered; but the public works raise the tax rates upon the people; thereupon the taxes are reduced by an attack upon the natianal bond-holders through the conversion of the five per cent. "rentes"* into four-and-halves. Yet the middle class must again be tipped: to this end, the tax on wine is doubled for the people, who buy it at retail, and is reduced to one-half for the middle class, that drink it at wholesale. Genuine labor organizations are dissolved, but promises are made of future wonders to accrue from organization. The farmers are to be helped: mortgage-banks are set up that must promote the indebtedness of the farmer and the concentration of property; but again, these banks are to be utilized especially to the end of squeezing money out of the confiscated estates of the House of Orleans; no capitalist will listen to this scheme, which, moreover, is not mentioned in the decree; the mortgage bank remains a mere decree, etc., etc.

Bonaparte would like to appear as the patriarchal benefactor of all classes: but he can give to none without taking from the others. As was said of the Duke of Guise, at the time of the Fronde, that he was the most obliging man in France because he had converted all his estates into bonds upon himself for his Parisians, so would Napoleon like to be the most obliging man in France and convert all property and all labor of France into a personal bond upon himself. He would like to steal the whole of France to make a present thereof to France, or rather to be able to purchase France back again with French money;—as chief of the "Society of December 10," he must purchase that which is to be his. All the State institutions, the Senate, the Council of

---

* The name of the French national bonds.

State, the Legislature, the Legion of Honor, the Soldiers' decorations, the public baths, the public buildings, the railroads, the General Staff of the National Guard, exclusive of the rank and file, the confiscated estates of the House of Orleans, —all are converted into institutions for purchase and sale. Every place in the Army and the machinery of Government becomes a purchasing power. The most important thing, however, in this process, whereby France is taken to be given back to herself, are the percentages that, in the transfer, drop into the hands of the chief and the members of the "Society of December 10." The witticisms with which the Countess of L., the mistress of de Morny, characterized the confiscations of the Orleanist estates: "C'est le premier vol de l'aigle,"[10] fits every flight of the eagle that is rather a crow. He himself and his followers daily call out to themselves, like the Italian Carthusian monk in the legend does to the miser, who displayfully counted the goods on which he could live for many years to come: "Tu fai conto sopra i beni, bisogna prima far il conto sopra gli anni."[11] In order not to make a mistake in the years, they count by minutes. A crowd of fellows, of the best among whom all that can be said is that one knows not whence he comes—a noisy, restless "Bohème," greedy after plunder, that crawls about in gallooned frocks with the same grotesque dignity as Soulonque's[12] Imperial dignitaries—, thronged the court, crowded the min-

---

[10] "It is the first flight of the eagle." The French word "vol" means theft as well as flight.

[11] "You count your property, you should rather count the years left to you."

[12] Soulonque was the negro Emperor of the shortlived negro Empire of Hayti.

istries, and pressed upon the head of the Government and of the Army. One can picture to himself this upper crust of the "Society of December 10" by considering that Véron Crevel" is their preacher of morality, and Granier de Cassagnac their thinker. When Guizot, at the time he was Minister, employed this Granier on an obscure sheet against the dynastic opposition, he used to praise him with the term: "C'est le roi des drôles." It were a mistake to recall the days of the Regency or of Louis XV. by the court and the kit of Louis Bonaparte's: "Often did France have a mistress-administration, but never yet an administration of kept men."[15]

Harassed by the contradictory demands of his situation, and compelled, like a sleight-of-hands performer, to keep, by means of constant surprises, the eyes of the public riveted upon himself as the substitute of Napoleon, compelled, consequently, every day to accomplish a sort of "coup" on a small scale, Bonaparte throws the whole bourgeois social system into disorder; he broaches everything that seemed unbroachable by the revolution of 1848; he makes one set of people patient under the revolution, and another anxious for it; and he produces anarchy itself in the name of order, by rubbing off from the whole machinery of Government the veneer of sanctity, by profanating it, by rendering it at once nauseating and laughable. He rehearses in Paris the cult of the sacred coat of Trier with the cult

[13] Crevel is a character of Balzac, drawn after Dr. Véron, the proprietor of the "Constitutional" newspaper, as a type of the dissolute Parisian Philistine.

[14] "He is the king of the clowns."

[15] Madame de Girardin.

of the Napoleonic Imperial mantle. But, when
the Imperial Mantle shall have finally fallen upon
the shoulders of Louis Bonaparte, then will also
the iron statue of Napoleon drop down from the
top of the Vendôme column.[16]

---

[16] A prophecy that a few years later, after Bonaparte's
coronation as Emperor, was literally fulfilled. By order of
the Emperor Louis Napoleon, the military statue of the
first Napoleon that originally surmounted the Vendome
column, was taken down and replaced by one of first Napoleon in imperial robes.

[THE END.]

www.bookjungle.com email: sales@bookjungle.com fax: 630-214-0564 mail: Book Jungle PO Box 2226 Champaign, IL 61825

The Two Babylons
Alexander Hislop

You may be surprised to learn that many traditions of Roman Catholicism in fact don't come from Christ's teachings but from an ancient Babylonian "Mystery" religion that was centered on Nimrod, his wife Semiramis, and a child Tammuz. This book shows how this ancient religion transformed itself as it incorporated Christ into its teachings ...

Religion/History   Pages:358

ISBN: *1-59462-010-5*   *MSRP $22.95*

QTY

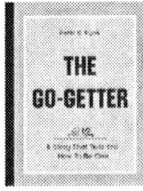

The Go-Getter
Kyne B. Peter

The Go Getter is the story of William Peck. He was a war veteran and amputee who will not be refused what he wants. Peck not only fights to find employment but continually proves himself more than competent at the many difficult test that are throw his way in the course of his early days with the Ricks Lumber Company ...

Business/Self Help/Inspirational   Pages:68

ISBN: *1-59462-186-1*   *MSRP $8.95*

QTY

The Power Of Concentration
Theron Q. Dumont

It is of the utmost value to learn how to concentrate. To make the greatest success of anything you must be able to concentrate your entire thought upon the idea you are working on. The person that is able to concentrate utilizes all constructive thoughts and shuts out all destructive ones...

Self Help/Inspirational   Pages:196

ISBN: *1-59462-141-1*   *MSRP $14.95*

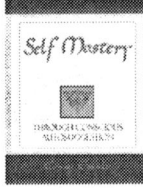

Self Mastery
Emile Coue

Emile Coue came up with novel way to improve the lives of people. He was a pharmacist by trade and often saw ailing people. This lead him to develop autosuggestion, a form of self-hypnosis. At the time his theories weren't popular but over the years evidence is mounting that he was indeed right all along ..

New Age/Self Help   Pages:98

ISBN: *1-59462-189-6*   *MSRP $7.95*

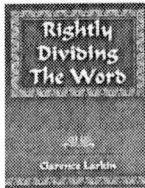

Rightly Dividing The Word
Clarence Larkin

The "Fundamental Doctrines" of the Christian Faith are clearly outlined in numerous books on Theology, but they are not available to the average reader and were mainly written for students. The Author has made it the work of his ministry to preach the "Fundamental Doctrines." To this end he has aimed to express them in the simplest and clearest manner.

Religion   Pages:352

ISBN: *1-59462-334-1*   *MSRP $23.45*

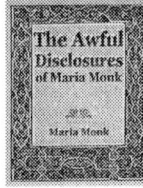

The Awful Disclosures Of
Maria Monk

"I cannot banish the scenes and characters of this book from my memory. To me it can never appear like an amusing fable, or lose its interest and importance. The story is one which is continually before me, and must return fresh to my mind with painful emotions as long as I live..."

Religion   Pages:232

ISBN: *1-59462-160-8*   *MSRP $17.95*

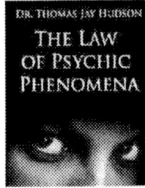

The Law of Psychic Phenomena
Thomson Jay Hudson

"I do not expect this book to stand upon its literary merits; for if it is unsound in principle, felicity of diction cannot save it, and if sound, homeliness of expression cannot destroy it. My primary object in offering it to the public is to assist in bringing Psychology within the domain of the exact sciences. That this has never been accomplished..."

New Age   Pages:420

ISBN: *1-59462-124-1*   *MSRP $29.95*

As a Man Thinketh
James Allen

"This little volume (the result of meditation and experience) is not intended as an exhaustive treatise on the much-written-upon subject of the power of thought. It is suggestive rather than explanatory, its object being to stimulate men and women to the discovery and perception of the truth that by virtue of the thoughts which they choose and encourage. "

Inspirational/Self Help   Pages:80

ISBN: *1-59462-231-0*   *MSRP $9.45*

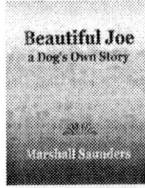

Beautiful Joe
Marshall Saunders

When Marshall visited the Moore family in 1892, she discovered Joe, a dog they had nursed back to health from his previous abusive home to live a happy life. So moved was she, that she wrote this classic masterpiece which won accolades and was recognized as a heartwarming symbol for humane animal treatment...

Fiction   Pages:256

ISBN: *1-59462-261-2*   *MSRP $18.45*

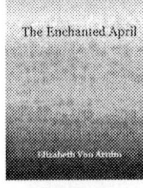

The Enchanted April
Elizabeth Von Arnim

It began in a woman's club in London on a February afternoon, an uncomfortable club, and a miserable afternoon when Mrs. Wilkins, who had come down from Hampstead to shop and had lunched at her club, took up The Times from the table in the smoking-room...

Fiction   Pages:368

ISBN: *1-59462-150-0*   *MSRP $23.45*

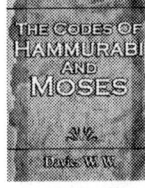

The Codes Of Hammurabi And
Moses - W. W. Davies

The discovery of the Hammurabi Code is one of the greatest achievements of archaeology, and is of paramount interest, not only to the student of the Bible, but also to all those interested in ancient history...

Religion   Pages:132

ISBN: *1-59462-338-4*   *MSRP $12.95*

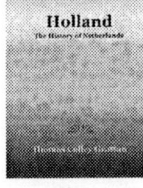

Holland - The History Of Netherlands
Thomas Colley Grattan

Thomas Grattan was a prestigious writer from Dublin who served as British Consul to the US. Among his works is an authoritative look at the history of Holland. A colorful and interesting look at history....

History/Politics   Pages:408

ISBN: *1-59462-137-3*   *MSRP $26.95*

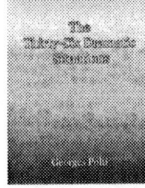

The Thirty-Six Dramatic Situations
Georges Polti

An incredibly useful guide for aspiring authors and playwrights. This volume categorizes every dramatic situation which could occur in a story and describes them in a list of 36 situations. A great aid to help inspire or formalize the creative writing process...

Self Help/Reference   Pages:204

ISBN: *1-59462-134-9*   *MSRP $15.95*

A Concise Dictionary of Middle English
A. L. Mayhew
Walter W. Skeat

The present work is intended to meet, in some measure, the requirements of those who wish to make some study of Middle-English, and who find a difficulty in obtaining such assistance as will enable them to find out the meanings and etymologies of the words most essential to their purpose ...

Reference/History   Pages:332

ISBN: *1-59462-119-5*   *MSRP $29.95*

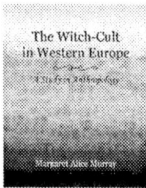

The Witch-Cult in Western Europe
Margaret Murray
The mass of existing material on this subject is so great that I have not attempted to make a survey of the whole of European "Witchcraft" but have confined myself to an intensive study of the cult in Great Britain. In order, however, to obtain a clearer understanding of the ritual and beliefs I have had recourse to French and Flemish sources...

Occult   Pages:308
ISBN: *1-59462-126-8*   MSRP *$22.45*

The Science Of Psychic Healing
Yogi Ramacharaka
This book is not a book of theories it deals with facts. Its author regards the best of theories as but working hypotheses to be used only until better ones present themselves. The "fact" is the principal thing the essential thing to uncover which the tool, theory, is used...

New Age/Health   Pages:180
ISBN: *1-59462-140-3*   MSRP *$13.95*

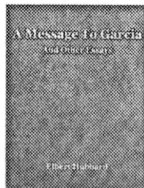

Bible Myths
Thomas Doane
In pursuing the study of the Bible Myths, facts pertaining thereto, in a condensed form, seemed to be greatly needed, and nowhere to be found. Widely scattered through hundreds of ancient and modern volumes, most of the contents of this book may herein be found; but any previous attempt to trace exclusively the myths and legends. .

Religion/History   Pages:644
ISBN: *1-59462-163-2*   MSRP *$38.95*

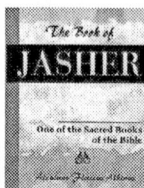

Tertium Organum
P. D. Ouspensky
A truly mind expanding writing that combines science with mysticism with unprecedented elegance. He presents the world we live in as a multi dimensional world and time as a motion through this world. But this isn't a cold and purely analytical explanation but a masterful presentation filled with similes and analogies...

New Age   Pages:356
ISBN: *1-59462-205-1*   MSRP *$23.95*

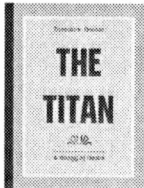

Advance Course in Yogi Philosophy
Yogi Ramacharaka
"The twelve lessons forming this volume were originally issued in the shape of monthly lessons, known as "The Advanced Course in Yogi Philosophy and Oriental Occultism" during a period of twelve months beginning with October, 1904, and ending September, 1905."

Philosophy/Inspirational/Self Help   Pages:340
ISBN: *1-59462-229-9*   MSRP *$22.95*

Ambassador Morgenthau's Story
Henry Morgenthau
"By this time the American people have probably become convinced that the Germans deliberately planned the conquest of the world. Yet they hesitate to convict on circumstantial evidence and for this reason all eye witnesses to this, the greatest crime in modern history, should volunteer their testimony..."

History   Pages:472
ISBN: *1-59462-244-2*   MSRP *$29.95*

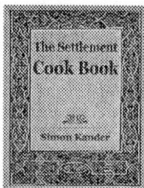

The Aquarian Gospel of Jesus the Christ
Levi Dowling
A retelling of Jesus' story which tells us what happened during the twenty year gap left by the Bible's New Testament. It tells of his travels to the far-east where he studied with the masters and fought against the rigid caste system. This book has enjoyed a resurgence in modern America and provides spiritual insight with charm. Its influences can be seen throughout the Age of Aquarius.

Religion   Pages:264
ISBN: *1-59462-321-X*   MSRP *$18.95*

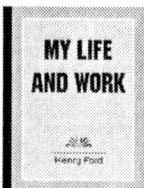

Philosophy Of Natural Therapeutics
Henry Lindlahr
We invite the earnest cooperation in this great work of all those who have awakened to the necessity for more rational living and for radical reform in healing methods...

Health/Philosophy/Self Help   Pages:552
ISBN: *1-59462-132-2*   MSRP *$34.95*

A Message to Garcia
Elbert Hubbard
This literary trifle, A Message to Garcia, was written one evening after supper, in a single hour. It was on the Twenty-second of February, Eighteen Hundred Ninety-nine, Washington's Birthday, and we were just going to press with the March Philistine...

New Age/Fiction   Pages:92
ISBN: *1-59462-144-6*   MSRP *$9.95*

The Book of Jasher
Alcuinus Flaccus Albinus
The Book of Jasher is an historical religious volume that many consider as a missing holy book from the Old Testament. Particularly studied by the Church of Later Day Saints and historians, it covers the history of the world from creation until the period of Judges in Israel. Its authenticity is bolstered due to a reference to the Book of Jasher in the Bible in Joshua 10:13

Religion/History   Pages:276
ISBN: *1-59462-197-7*   MSRP *$18.95*

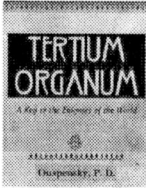

The Titan
Theodore Dreiser
"When Frank Algernon Cowperwood emerged from the Eastern District Penitentiary, in Philadelphia he realized that the old life he had lived in that city since boyhood was ended. His youth was gone, and with it had been lost the great business prospects of his earlier manhood. He must begin again..."

Fiction   Pages:564
ISBN: *1-59462-220-5*   MSRP *$33.95*

Biblical Essays
J. B. Lightfoot
About one-third of the present volume has already seen the light. The opening essay "On the Internal Evidence for the Authenticity and Genuineness of St John's Gospel" was published in the "Expositor" in the early months of 1890, and has been reprinted since...

Religion/History   Pages:480
ISBN: *1-59462-238-8*   MSRP *$30.95*

The Settlement Cook Book
Simon Kander
A legacy from the civil war, this book is a classic "American charity cookbook," which was used for fundraisers starting in Milwaukee. While it has transformed over the years, this printing provides great recipes from American history. Over two million copies have been sold. This volume contains a rich collection of recipes from noted chefs and hostesses of the turn of the century...

How-to   Pages:472
ISBN: *1-59462-256-6*   MSRP *$29.95*

My Life and Work
Henry Ford
Henry Ford revolutionized the world with his implementation of mass production for the Model T automobile. Gain valuable business insight into his life and work with his own auto-biography... "We have only started on our development of our country we have not as yet, with all our talk of wonderful progress, done more than scratch the surface. The progress has been wonderful enough but..."

Biographies/History/Business   Pages:300
ISBN: *1-59462-198-5*   MSRP *$21.95*

QTY

☐	**The Rosicrucian Cosmo-Conception Mystic Christianity** *by Max Heindel* — **ISBN: 1-59462-188-8 $38.95**

The Rosicrucian Cosmo-conception is not dogmatic, neither does it appeal to any other authority than the reason of the student. It is: not controversial, but is: sent forth in the, hope that it may help to clear..   New Age/Religion Pages 646

☐ **Abandonment To Divine Providence** *by Jean-Pierre de Caussade*   **ISBN: 1-59462-228-0 $25.95**
"The Rev. Jean Pierre de Caussade was one of the most remarkable spiritual writers of the Society of Jesus in France in the 18th Century. His death took place at Toulouse in 1751. His works have gone through many editions and have been republished...   Inspirational/Religion Pages 400

☐ **Mental Chemistry** *by Charles Haanel*   **ISBN: 1-59462-192-6 $23.95**
Mental Chemistry allows the change of material conditions by combining and appropriately utlizing the power of the mind. Much like applied chemistry creates something new and unique out of careful combinations of chemicals the mastery of mental chemistry..   New Age Pages 354

☐ **The Letters of Robert Browning and Elizabeth Barret Barrett 1845-1846 vol II**   **ISBN: 1-59462-193-4 $35.95**
by Robert Browning and Elizabeth Barrett   Biographies Pages 596

☐ **Gleanings In Genesis (volume I)** *by Arthur W. Pink*   **ISBN: 1-59462-130-6 $27.45**
Appropriately has Genesis been termed "the seed plot of the Bible" for in it we have, in germ form, almost all of the great doctrines which are afterwards fully developed in the books of Scripture which follow...   Religion/Inspirational Pages 420

☐ **The Master Key** *by L. W. de Laurence*   **ISBN: 1-59462-001-6 $30.95**
In no branch of human knowledge has there been a more lively increase of the spirit of research during the past few years than in the study of Psychology, Concentration and Mental Discipline. The requests for authentic lessons in Thought Control, Mental Discipline and...   New Age/Business Pages 422

☐ **The Lesser Key Of Solomon Goetia** *by L. W. de Laurence*   **ISBN: 1-59462-092-X $9.95**
This translation of the first book of the "Lernegton" which is now for the first time made accessible to students of Talismanic Magic was done, after careful collation and edition, from numerous Ancient Manuscripts in Hebrew, Latin, and French...   New Age/Occult Pages 92

☐ **Rubaiyat Of Omar Khayyam** *by Edward Fitzgerald*   **ISBN: 1-59462-332-5 $13.95**
Edward Fitzgerald, whom the world has already learned, in spite of his own efforts to remain within the shadow of anonymity, to look upon as one of the rarest poets of the century, was born at Bredfield, in Suffolk, on the 31st of March, 1809. He was the third son of John Purcell...   Music Pages 172

☐ **Ancient Law** *by Henry Maine*   **ISBN: 1-59462-128-4 $29.95**
The chief object of the following pages is to indicate some of the earliest ideas of mankind, as they are reflected in Ancient Law, and to point out the relation of those ideas to modern thought.   Religion/History Pages 452

☐ **Far-Away Stories** *by William J. Locke*   **ISBN: 1-59462-129-2 $19.45**
"Good wine needs no bush, but a collection of mixed vintages does. And this book is just such a collection. Some of the stories I do not want to remain buried for ever in the museum files of dead magazine-numbers an author's not unpardonable vanity..."   Fiction Pages 272

☐ **Life of David Crockett** *by David Crockett*   **ISBN: 1-59462-250-7 $27.45**
"Colonel David Crockett was one of the most remarkable men of the times in which he lived. Born in humble life, but gifted with a strong will, an indomitable courage, and unremitting perseverance...   Biographies/New Age Pages 424

☐ **Lip-Reading** *by Edward Nitchie*   **ISBN: 1-59462-206-X $25.95**
Edward B. Nitchie, founder of the New York School for the Hard of Hearing, now the Nitchie School of Lip-Reading, Inc. wrote "LIP-READING Principles and Practice". The development and perfecting of this meritorious work on lip-reading was an undertaking...   How-to Pages 400

☐ **A Handbook of Suggestive Therapeutics, Applied Hypnotism, Psychic Science**   **ISBN: 1-59462-214-0 $24.95**
by Henry Munro   Health/New Age/Health/Self-help Pages 376

☐ **A Doll's House: and Two Other Plays** *by Henrik Ibsen*   **ISBN: 1-59462-112-8 $19.95**
Henrik Ibsen created this classic when in revolutionary 1848 Rome. Introducing some striking concepts in playwriting for the realist genre, this play has been studied the world over.   Fiction/Classics/Plays 308

☐ **The Light of Asia** *by sir Edwin Arnold*   **ISBN: 1-59462-204-3 $13.95**
In this poetic masterpiece, Edwin Arnold describes the life and teachings of Buddha. The man who was to become known as Buddha to the world was born as Prince Gautama of India but he rejected the worldly riches and abandoned the reigns of power when...   Religion/History/Biographies Pages 170

☐ **The Complete Works of Guy de Maupassant** *by Guy de Maupassant*   **ISBN: 1-59462-157-8 $16.95**
"For days and days, nights and nights, I had dreamed of that first kiss which was to consecrate our engagement, and I knew not on what spot I should put my lips..."   Fiction/Classics Pages 240

☐ **The Art of Cross-Examination** *by Francis L. Wellman*   **ISBN: 1-59462-309-0 $26.95**
Written by a renowned trial lawyer, Wellman imparts his experience and uses case studies to explain how to use psychology to extract desired information through questioning.   How-to/Science/Reference Pages 408

☐ **Answered or Unanswered?** *by Louisa Vaughan*   **ISBN: 1-59462-248-5 $10.95**
Miracles of Faith in China   Religion Pages 112

☐ **The Edinburgh Lectures on Mental Science (1909)** *by Thomas*   **ISBN: 1-59462-008-3 $11.95**
This book contains the substance of a course of lectures recently given by the writer in the Queen Street Hall, Edinburgh. Its purpose is to indicate the Natural Principles governing the relation between Mental Action and Material Conditions...   New Age/Psychology Pages 148

☐ **Ayesha** *by H. Rider Haggard*   **ISBN: 1-59462-301-5 $24.95**
Verily and indeed it is the unexpected that happens! Probably if there was one person upon the earth from whom the Editor of this, and of a certain previous history, did not expect to hear again...   Classics Pages 380

☐ **Ayala's Angel** *by Anthony Trollope*   **ISBN: 1-59462-352-X $29.95**
The two girls were both pretty, but Lucy who was twenty-one who supposed to be simple and comparatively unattractive, whereas Ayala was credited, as her Bombwhat romantic name might show, with poetic charm and a taste for romance. Ayala when her father died was nineteen...   Fiction Pages 484

☐ **The American Commonwealth** *by James Bryce*   **ISBN: 1-59462-286-8 $34.45**
An interpretation of American democratic political theory. It examines political mechanics and society from the perspective of Scotsman James Bryce   Politics Pages 572

☐ **Stories of the Pilgrims** *by Margaret P. Pumphrey*   **ISBN: 1-59462-116-0 $17.95**
This book explores pilgrims religious oppression in England as well as their escape to Holland and eventual crossing to America on the Mayflower, and their early days in New England...   History Pages 268

Bringing Classics to Life

BOOK JUNGLE

www.bookjungle.com *email: sales@bookjungle.com fax: 630-214-0564 mail: Book Jungle PO Box 2226 Champaign, IL 61825*

QTY

The Fasting Cure *by Sinclair Upton*   ISBN: *1-59462-222-1* **$13.95**
In the Cosmopolitan Magazine for May, 1910, and in the Contemporary Review (London) for April, 1910, I published an article dealing with my experiences in fasting. I have written a great many magazine articles, but never one which attracted so much attention... New Age/Self Help/Health Pages 164

Hebrew Astrology *by Sepharial*   ISBN: *1-59462-308-2* **$13.45**
In these days of advanced thinking it is a matter of common observation that we have left many of the old landmarks behind and that we are now pressing forward to greater heights and to a wider horizon than that which represented the mind-content of our progenitors... Astrology Pages 144

Thought Vibration or The Law of Attraction in the Thought World   ISBN: *1-59462-127-6* **$12.95**
by William Walker Atkinson   Psychology/Religion Pages 144

Optimism *by Helen Keller*   ISBN: *1-59462-108-X* **$15.95**
Helen Keller was blind, deaf, and mute since 19 months old, yet famously learned how to overcome these handicaps, communicate with the world, and spread her lectures promoting optimism. An inspiring read for everyone... Biographies/Inspirational Pages 84

Sara Crewe *by Frances Burnett*   ISBN: *1-59462-360-0* **$9.45**
In the first place, Miss Minchin lived in London. Her home was a large, dull, tall one, in a large, dull square, where all the houses were alike, and all the sparrows were alike, and where all the door-knockers made the same heavy sound... Childrens/Classic Pages 88

The Autobiography of Benjamin Franklin *by Benjamin Franklin*   ISBN: *1-59462-135-7* **$24.95**
The Autobiography of Benjamin Franklin has probably been more extensively read than any other American historical work, and no other book of its kind has had such ups and downs of fortune. Franklin lived for many years in England, where he was agent... Biographies/History Pages 332

Name	
Email	
Telephone	
Address	
City, State ZIP	

☐ **Credit Card**   ☐ **Check / Money Order**

Credit Card Number	
Expiration Date	
Signature	

Please Mail to: Book Jungle
PO Box 2226
Champaign, IL 61825
or Fax to: 630-214-0564

ORDERING INFORMATION

web: *www.bookjungle.com*
email: *sales@bookjungle.com*
fax: *630-214-0564*
mail: *Book Jungle PO Box 2226 Champaign, IL 61825*
or PayPal *to sales@bookjungle.com*

Please contact us for bulk discounts

DIRECT-ORDER TERMS

**20% Discount if You Order
Two or More Books**
Free Domestic Shipping!
Accepted: Master Card, Visa,
Discover, American Express

Printed in the United Kingdom
by Lightning Source UK Ltd.
119534UK00001B/212

9 781594 623769